Faster &
Faster

GW00673266

Bob Fisher began sailing at the age of two from the east coast fishing village of Brightlingsea. He progressed from dinghy racing, where he won four world championships, a European championship and twelve national championships to offshore racing. He has raced successfully in all the world's major offshore races, culminating with RORC championship win in a season in which his *Barracuda of Tarrant* was yacht of the year.

For 30 years Bob Fisher has been a full time sailing journalist writing for *The Guardian*, *The Observer* and *Yachts & Yachting* as well as contributing to a dozen magazines around the world. He is author of 19 books on sailing.

Barry Pickthall began sailing at the age of 13. For the past 22 years he has covered the world's major yachting events, and in particular has a long and close association with the Whitbread Round The World Race. As well as reporting on it world-wide, he has been shore manager for Cornelis van Rietschoten's *Flyer*, the winning yacht in the 1981-82 race, and Eric Tabarly's *Cote d'Or* in the 1985-86 event. Barry Pickthall heads PPL, the official photo agency for the race, with over 2 million sailing pictures in the library.

Barry Pickthall is *The Times* yachting correspondent, European correspondent for *Yachting* magazine (USA) and writes for over a dozen magazines world-wide. He is author of eight widely varied maritime titles.

Faster &
Faster

Bob Fisher & Barry Pickthall

ADLARD COLES NAUTICAL
London

Published 1994 by Adlard Coles Nautical
an imprint of A & C Black (Publishers) Ltd
35 Bedford Row, London WC1R 4JH

First edition 1994

ISBN 0-7136-4089-8

A CIP catalogue record for this book is available from the British Library.

Typeset in 9½ on 11pt Linotron Palatino by Falcon Graphic Arts, Wallington, Surrey.

Printed and bound in Great Britain by
Butler & Tanner Ltd, Frome and London

The views expressed in this book are those of the authors, and not
necessarily those of Whitbread PLC or the Race Organisers.

Contents

Acknowledgements

The authors wish to thank all the competitors for their tolerance and forebearance when answering our questions during the course of the race. It has greatly helped in our reportage in this book of what went on when we could not be there.

This book would not have been possible within the timescale which we believed was essential for its commercial success without the dedicated assistance of Rachel Nuding. Our apologies go to her children for 'stealing' their mother for a whole weekend in order that the tight production schedule could be met, and our thanks to her for giving so freely of her time and for her patience in deciphering exactly what we meant, either on handwritten scraps of corrected paper or on the electronic medium we chose to use.

The Monstas of Mark O'Brien, the official cartoonist for the 1993/94 Whitbread Race, have enlivened our days and we are grateful for the use of some to lighten our text. The same is true for the photographs of Mark Pepper, a man who is happiest close to the action, either on the water or dangling from a helicopter. Full marks to both of them

Carole Edwards, our editor, dealt with the problems of two peripatetic authors eager to be elsewhere with aplomb. She deserves a medal.

We would also like to thank the Whitbread Race Office staff for all their help and continued support. Ian Bailey-Willmot and those who have travelled with the race, as well as those who have been left behind, have done everything in their power to make this book possible.

Our thanks also to Nikon for their Coolscan and LS3510 picture scanners, BT for their ISDN data lines, SCii and 4-Sight for their ISDN computer cards and software, and Whitbread for their overall support in developing PPL's Whitbread remote access Imagebase.

BT's remarkable results service has been a godsend to us and our fellow journalists, and we particularly wish to thank both Edward Scott and David Mitchelson for so rapidly rallying to our cause with the position charts which appear in this book.

Finally, to Sally and Dee for their understanding when we have worked odd hours, become irritable, and pleaded unavailability when there were domestic duties to be done.

Bob Fisher, Lymington
Barry Pickthall, Littlehampton
13 June 1994

1

Two decades of Whitbread history

I t all began in 1971, when an idea from Anthony Churchill and Guy Pearse was circulated among yachtsmen and the press at Cowes Week. A fully crewed ocean race around the world in four stages was something very different to all that had gone before in the sport. Yachtsmen loved the idea but the two promoters failed to attract the necessary sponsorship to finance the race and handed it over to the Royal Naval Sailing Association in the following year. It was the RNSA, who already had entered negotiations with Whitbread, who found the effort and financial support to run this ocean marathon.

The first race started on 8 September 1973, when 17 yachts from seven nations answered the starting canon at Southsea Castle, which was fired by Sir Alec Rose. Those 17 boats were as diverse as could possibly be imagined, ranging from Eric Tabarly's *Pen Duick VI*, a 73 ft alloy ketch with a spent uranium keel specially built for the race, to the 1936 yawl *Peter von Danzig*. Some were stock designs, including the eventual winner, the Swan 65 ketch *Sayula II* owned by Ramon Carlin, a Mexican entrepreneur.

The race was one of distinct highs and lows, endorsing the concept that survival was of equal importance to speed. *Pen Duick VI* started favourite but lost her mast on two occasions; *Adventure*, the Royal Navy's Nicholson 55 won three of the four legs, but a broken rudder on the second leg ruined her chances. Three men tragically lost their lives in the Southern Ocean, in latitudes where no man had raced yachts before. Aboard one of the competing yachts was a 25 -year-old sailor who was to make the Whitbread his own endeavour; his name was Peter Blake.

First to finish on 11 April was Chay Blyth and his crew from the Parachute Regiment in an Alan Gurney designed 73 ft ketch, *Great Britain II*, personally funded by 'Union Jack' Hayward. It was not quite good enough for her to win the leg, that was *Adventure*'s honour, neither did it win her the race on corrected time, for when *Sayula II* finished on Easter Day, she took the major prize for winning the race on corrected time. But only just – her forestay had all but parted earlier on the leg and only the ingenuity of her crew had turned possible disaster into victory.

There was no doubting the overall success of the race, but the organisers realised that some alterations would have to be made, even if only minor, before the race was run again in four years time. Auckland replaced Sydney as the second stopover, but the decision was made to continue with Cape Town and Rio de Janeiro. Despite huge interest in the race, only 15 boats crossed the starting line.

Tabarly was back with *Pen Duick VI*, as was *Great Britain II*, this time skippered by Rob James with 16 fare paying charterers as crew. *Adventure* also raced again as did Les Williams with another Maxi, this time the 77 ft *Heath's Condor* which he shared with Robin Knox-Johnston; Blake went with them as a watch leader. In the wake of *Sayula II*'s success, there were three Swan 65's: Pierre Felhmann in his first Whitbread had *Disque d'Or*, Clare Francis, the first female skipper, with *ADC Accutrac* and Nick Ratcliffe's sloop-rigged *Kings Legend*. The ketch rig was still much favoured, particularly by Cornelis van Rietschoten, a Dutchman who asked Sparkman and Stephens to improve on the Swan 65 design and built *Flyer* in aluminium.

There was plenty of innovation among the fleet, notably a carbon fibre mast on *Heath's Condor*, but this was a last minute improvement to the boat which failed just 3,000 miles out of Portsmouth. *Heath's Condor* headed for Monrovia to meet up with an air freighted aluminium alloy replacement and only just made Cape Town in time to start the second stage. *Flyer* had a two hour advantage over *Kings Legend* on corrected time at the start of the second leg but the Swan 65 was soon 300 miles ahead. Rudder delamination problems made *Kings Legend* slow and she finished 45 minutes ahead into Auckland.

Auckland proved a great choice as a stopover port, its sail-crazy citizens rallying to support the race, the boats and the crews giving the race a great send off. On the next leg, a navigational mistake by *Kings Legend* virtually handed the race on a plate to *Flyer*. Rio was not everything that the sailors might have desired – bribes were necessary to clear sails from Customs and Clare Francis's conga at the Yacht Club ended with the riot police flailing truncheons and firing tear gas at the crews.

Rob James and his 'passengers' posted a new race record for elapsed time, which was 10 days shorter than Chay Blyth and his paratroopers had set four years earlier. *Kings Legend* beat *Flyer* to Portsmouth but only by an hour and 20 minutes, so that van Rietschoten became the winner of the second Whitbread race with *Flyer*.

When the fleet came to the line for the start of the third Whitbread, it was of record size – 29 yachts from 15 countries answered the starter's gun with many old faces among them, though only 20 completed all four legs. Cornelis van Rietschoten had a new *Flyer*, this one a Maxi, 76 ft long designed by German Frers and it was to receive stiff competition from Peter Blake with the Farr designed *Ceramco New Zealand*. This 68 footer was designed and built after Blake had appealed to key business and sailing friends in his home country.

Great Britain II was back in the name of *United Friendly*, with Chay Blyth in command while Les Williams had built himself an 80 ft Maxi, *FCF Challenger*. Tabarly led the French with his 73 footer, renamed *Euromarché*; he was joined by Alain Gabbay with the 66 ft *Charles Heidsieck III* and André Viant with the 62 ft *Kriter IX*. Felhmann had a Farr designed 58 footer, *Disque d'Or III* and Digby Taylor brought the rival Davidson designed 50 ft *Outward Bound* from New Zealand. Padda Kuttel entered a Swan 65, *Xargo III*, from South Africa while the original *Flyer*, re-rigged as a sloop, was entered by Neil Bergt as *Alaska Eagle*.

Blake's challenge received a major setback 150 miles north of Ascension Island when the mast broke 16 feet above the deck. With remarkable Kiwi ingenuity, Blake and the crew utilised the top section (salvaged along with the mainsail) and taking the westerly route around the South Atlantic high, arrived in Cape Town a little less than 11 days behind *Flyer*. Van Reitschoten's idea had been to win every leg on the water – being first home appealed to him and he was not looking for handicap honours. Nevertheless, he was third behind *Kriter IX* and *Charles Heidsieck III*.

The leg to Auckland was a tremendous battle between *Flyer* and *Ceramco*. Blake was determined to do everything in his power to be first into his home port and the two skippers slugged it out, toe to toe, for most of the way. Somewhat inevitably,

Flyer made it, but only by eight hours; Blake, however, won the leg on corrected time with *Charles Heidsieck* second and *Flyer* again third. Blake, however, had been unaware that, during the leg, van Rietschoten had a suffered an attack of angina which led to the Dutch skipper having a heart attack. His crew wanted to divert to Fremantle, but van Rietschoten wouldn't hear of it. He insisted the boat kept racing and that silence about his condition be maintained, because he said, 'if they had known I had a health problem, the Kiwis would have pushed their boat even harder.'

The duel continued on the third leg, each skipper wanting to be first around Cape Horn. *Ceramco* gained the initial advantage from a more southerly route but *Flyer* struck back, including a day's run of 327 miles, a new Whitbread record. Eventually *Flyer* beat *Ceramco* to the bottom of South America by just five miles. Even then the race was not over. After rounding into the Atlantic, a windshift gave *Ceramco* the lead but the longer waterline length of *Flyer* wore down the Kiwis on the leg north to Mar del Plata and *Flyer* finished seven hours ahead of *Ceramco*. It was, however, to be a small boat leg with Phillipe Poupon's *Mor'bihan* taking the handicap honours from *Charles Heidsieck III*.

The final leg from Mar del Plata was set to be a battle between *Charles Heidsieck III* and *Kriter IX* – just 11 hours separated them on corrected time with *Charles Heidsieck* having the advantage. *Flyer* was in third place in the overall standings, some 34 hours behind the leader. Nobody could have foreseen what was to happen.

When *Flyer* crossed the finishing line, *Charles Heidsieck* had only 600 miles to sail, which meant an average of 7.6 knots if the French boat were to win. It seemed that there was no doubt Gabbay would do so, but he forgot to cover the opposition. *Charles Heidsieck III* went to the east, anticipating the north-east trades and never saw the good reaching breezes which *Flyer* and *Ceramco* picked up at the Azores. For a long time the French yacht was parked with hardly any breeze and finished a little over five days behind *Flyer*. With *Kriter IX* another four hours further back, it gave the overall handicap prize to the Dutchman, who had, additionally, been first home on each of the four legs.

For Peter Blake and the crew of *Ceramco* there was consolation on winning the final leg on corrected time and there was little doubt in anyone's mind that the Farr designed 68 footer would have won this race on handicap but for her disastrous dismasting on the first leg.

Four years later, Blake was back on the scene with the Ron Holland designed Maxi-sloop, *Lion New Zealand*; she was one of seven Maxi-sized yachts challenging for line honours. Lion was a total re-think in concept by Blake who had not only the heaviest displacement yacht but also the biggest crew – 22 in number. He argued that *Flyer* could have been sailed much harder with a bigger crew.

Others asked Farr to develop the *Ceramco* theme, among them Pierre Felhmann with the 80 ft *UBS Switzerland*. She displaced 61,000 lb, 15,500 lb less than *Lion NZ*. The other Maxis included Eric Tabarly with the 83 ft *Côte d'Or* and *Drum*, a near sistership of *Lion NZ* owned by Simon Le Bon of the pop group Duran Duran. Drum's keel fell off shortly after the start of the Fastnet race, just eight weeks before the start of the Whitbread, and under Skip Novak, the crew helped to restore the boat to its former glory and be ready in time.

Tabarly was in a somewhat similar position having had only five months to build the Joubert/Nivelt design, and two months of sailing to develop her. *Atlantic Privateer*, another of the Farr designs, was Padda Kuttel's second shot at the race and was highly regarded by most as the strongest challenger. Only her mast was in doubt – a second-hand rig bought from *Flyer*, which probably had already done too many miles. The other Farr Maxi was *NZI Enterprise*, a low budget challenge from Digby Taylor of New Zealand.

There were several smaller boats which were likely contenders for handicap honours including the 58 ft *L'Esprit d'Equipe*, a Philippe Briand design with one Whitbread already under her belt as *33 Export*. Re-moulded by her designer she had finished second of the Whitbread contenders in the Fastnet race behind *Atlantic Privateer*. In all, 15 boats started the fourth Whitbread race.

The first leg will long be remembered for the sensational dismasting of the race leader, *Atlantic Privateer*. She had been pushed just too hard for the already tired spar to withstand the strain. Kuttel motored into Luderitz where a replacement made of welded waterpipe was stepped. It quickly failed. Others also had major repair problems by the time they reached Cape Town. *Drum*, with Lawrie Smith as a helmsman for this leg, had serious delamination problems as did *Côte d'Or* while *NZI Enterprise* had a huge bend in her mast.

Felhmann was first into port with *UBS*, a long way ahead of the opposition. The Swiss skipper was 16 hours in front of Blake and almost a whole day clear of Tabarly. *Drum* had been held back by her serious delamination and was only seventh to finish, but it was Lionel Pean with *L'Esprit d'Equipe* who took the handicap win from Dirk Nauta in *Philips Innovator*.

The Southern Ocean failed to deliver the strong running conditions for which it has been famous. The majority of the winds for the second leg were northerly and headsail reaching was the order of the day; while it may have been fast, it was also wet; penetratingly wet and cold.

Two yachts went into this leg knowing that the eyes of the world and particularly those of the Race committee would be upon them – *Côte d'Or* and *Drum*. The repairs to each of them had been significant and in the case of Tabarly's boat, a new keel had been fitted in addition to the repair work to the hull. *Atlantic Privateer* stepped a new mast and was soon contesting the lead. *Côte d'Or*'s crew discovered more delamination and for a while Tabarly considered heading for Fremantle but when conditions eased, he returned to an easterly heading.

The finish of that leg, into Auckland, was the closest ever between the leaders with *Atlantic Privateer* beating *NZI Enterprise* by seven minutes 20 seconds after a 200 mile head-to-head battle all the way down the North Island coast of New Zealand from Cape Reinga. *UBS Switzerland* was third to finish, just under two hours behind the leader followed by *Drum* and *Lion*. The leg however went, on handicap, to *Philips Innovator* who beat *L'Esprit d'Equipe* by a few minutes under a day. That put Nauta into the overall lead.

Digby Taylor's joy was relatively short lived. A few days into the third leg *NZI Enterprise* was close hauled on port tack in 25 knots of wind when her mast collapsed in three pieces. The race was over for Taylor and his crew, a great disappointment as they had proved they had the speed to match the best.

UBS was first to Cape Horn, but the pack was close behind as they began a slow leg north to Punta del Este. Two days from the finish, *UBS* managed only 129 miles in 24 hours but there was wind to come, plenty of it. The tail of a Pampero, a wind which originates in the South American mountains and rolls out to sea under a cigar shaped black cloud, can blow as much as 60 to 90 knots. This one was not quite that vicious but it brought *UBS* scurrying home 9 hours ahead of *Drum* with *Atlantic Privateer* 1 hour 20 minutes behind her. But it was to be a small boat bonanza once again with *L'Esprit d'Equipe* taking the handicap honours and retrieving the overall handicap position from *Philips Innovator* by nearly 5 hours.

The fourth leg began with a band playing on the quayside at Punta but the northerly breeze was a portent of what was to come. It was a hard slog up the Brazilian coast with *UBS* taking an early lead. *Lion* was in pursuit, locked in combat with *Drum* and *Côte d'Or*. *Atlantic Privateer* was also in the leaders' battle while behind them Lionel Pean struggled with *L'Esprit d'Equipe* to hold on to *Philips Innovator*, for it was between them that the Whitbread Race would be settled.

There seemed to be no holding Fehlmann. At his third attempt, the Swiss skipper eased away from his rivals to finish first by a margin of one day and 16 hours. It was all too easy, and he demonstrated the true commercialism behind the race as he sailed up The Solent peeling spinnaker after spinnaker to give exposure to each of his major sponsors. Audemars Piquet gave way to Union Bank of Switzerland; then came Alusuisse before the travel agents Fert. It was a great performance, eclipsed only by that of the yacht which took the line honours prize for total elapsed time by 4 days and 16 hours from Peter Blake's *Lion New Zealand*, in turn 12 hours ahead of *Drum*.

Almost four days after *UBS* had finished, Lionel Pean and his crew brought *L'Esprit d'Equipe* into Portsmouth in a time that was to give him another 17 hours over *Philips Innovator* so that at the end of the race, the Frenchman took the handicap prize by 22^1/2 hours.

The start of the fifth race, on 2 September 1989, saw 23 boats on starboard tack charging at the starting line in 12 knots of breeze. Around them was the biggest spectator fleet ever assembled for a yacht race in the UK, carrying an estimated 50,000 people. Certain changes had been wrought to the structure of the race, which encouraged 15 Maxis to race on level terms, without handicap. Two more elderly Maxis raced in a cruiser division while the rest were grouped in three handicap classes, among them the 58 ft *Maiden*, the first all-woman entry, skippered by Tracy Edwards.

Two of the Maxis, Peter Blake's *Steinlager 2* and Grant Dalton's *Fisher & Paykel*, sported modern ketch rigs. Both were Farr designed and the same rig option had been offered to Pierre Fehlmann for *Merit*, but he declined, believing that he had learned enough about ketches when sailing the Swan 65, *Disque d'Or* in the second race. It was decision that he was later to regret when the race developed into a battle between the two New Zealand twin-masters.

Blake took *Steinlager 2* further to the west than any of the other boats as he approached the Doldrums on the first leg and it was to prove a race-winning strategy, 'Big Red' as the ketch became known, had converged with Lawrie Smith's *Rothmans* off Cape Finisterre; *Steinlager 2* was setting an 85 percent spinnaker and reefed mainsail with nothing on the mizzen, while *Rothmans* had a poled-out headsail with a reefed main. The New Zealand ketch carried on out to sea while the British sloop went inshore. It was there that the move was made. Glen Sowry, then a trimmer on *Steinlager 2*, wrote at the time, 'This splitting of direction was to prove to be our big break on the rest of the fleet in this leg and ultimately the race.'

By the tenth day, Blake's lead over the other ketch was 270 miles, but a calm patch saw Fehlmann in Merit pull up to within 40 miles. When, two days later, *Steinlager 2* did hit the real Doldrums, she was through them very quickly in contrast to her rivals. Out to the west, the band of calms and squalls was narrow and once through them, *Steinlager 2* sped away to beat *Merit* into Punta del Este by almost 12 hours. *Fisher & Paykel* lost her mizzen mast in strong winds off Rio de Janeiro and was 31 hours behind the leader. *Rothmans* suffered structural damage to her deck and Smith and his crew had to nurse the Rob Humphreys' designed sloop into port three and a half hours behind *Fisher & Paykel*. On handicap, the smaller boats didn't have a look in.

The course for the race had been changed, taking into account the political situation in South Africa. The worsening of apartheid demanded that the Royal Naval Sailing Association cut Cape Town out of the stopover ports. But this would mean that the second leg would be particularly long and arduous: 7,650 miles across the Southern Ocean to Fremantle, another new port in Whitbread history. Grant Dalton was to lead for much of the leg with with *Fisher & Paykel*, but made the decision to head up from the southern latitudes too soon and was passed by *Steinlager 2*, *Rothmans* and *Merit*.

Steinlager 2 finished at dawn and an hour and a half later, a press of spectators were treated to a match race finish every bit as good as those which had taken place when the America's Cup was held on Gage Roads, between Fremantle and Rottnest Island. *Merit* came around the north end of Rottnest in the lead but Smith, who had coached the Kookaburra syndicate there two years earlier, was tactically superior and beat his rival to the finishing line by 28 seconds! Dalton, who had led for so long, was fourth – another hour and a half behind. *Steinlager 2*'s overall lead was increased.

The leg was notable for the performance of Tracy Edwards and the all-women crew of *Maiden*. They were 17th to finish, but more than a day ahead of *Rucanor Sport* and *L'Esprit de Liberté* (winner of the previous race under a new name and skipper, Patrick Tabarly). It lifted *Maiden* to be the overall leader in class D.

The leg was also notable for the disaster which hit *Creightons Naturally* at 0322 on Sunday 12 November. In big seas, the 80 ft boat gybed involuntarily and the running backstay broke causing the yacht to gybe again. The main sheet looped around two of the grinder pedestals and ripped them off the deck. As the mainsail was being taken down, the yacht was hit by two very large waves and the boat broached. Anthony Phillips and Bart van den Dwey were swept overboard. Both were wearing lifejackets equipped with flares and personal radio beacons. All sails were lowered and the boat motored back to where the men had gone overboard. Van den Dwey was sighted with the help of a white parachute flare and was recovered after 47 minutes in the water. He was successfully resuscitated. Phillips was next aboard and resuscitation attempts carried out for three hours were unsuccessful. It is believed that he hit one of the guard-rail stanchions as he went overboard and may have been unconscious in the water, which would account for his lifejacket not being inflated. Phillips was buried in the ocean that claimed his life.

The 3,434 mile leg to Auckland is a sprint in Whitbread terms and the two Kiwi ketches were to make it just that as they headed for home. The two took over the front running from the outset and were never very far apart, match racing all the way. Thirteen days into the race, they approached Cape Reinga and *Steinlager 2* led by 200 yards. There were 200 miles to go and the duel was fierce. Gybe followed gybe, matched and counter-matched and it was all settled when *Steinlager 2*'s navigator, Mike Quilter, heard a listener on Newstalk 1ZB mention on the radio that a front had just passed through taking much of the washing off the line. Blake prepared for the upcoming squall, with a small genoa on deck, ready to hoist and called for an early spinnaker drop when he saw the wind on the water ahead.

The result was that *Steinlager 2* was fully in control when the squall struck and the crew of *Fisher & Paykel* were caught unawares. Sowry reported that a smile crept over Blake's face and he was heard to utter, 'Got the bastards.' His preparedness put *Steinlager 2* a mile ahead and with less than 10 miles to go, there was no chance of '*Big Red*' being beaten. She finished across the line at Orakei Wharf six minutes clear. *Merit* and *Rothmans* had had a similar battle and this time it went to the Swiss skipper, ten minutes ahead of Smith, but an hour behind the leaders. Once again, *Maiden* claimed the honours in class D, beating six of the Maxis on corrected time as well. For her performance, Tracy Edwards received the British Yachtsman of the Year Award. Blake and his crew received the New Zealand equivalent; the Whitbread was seen to be a major force in the sport.

The restart from Auckland caused something of a minor sensation. It was a brilliant summer's day and everything that could get afloat was out there carrying Aucklanders to watch the boats leave. *The Card*, the third of the Farr ketches, skippered by Roger Nilson of Sweden, went into the spectator fleet and the rigging of her mizzen mast caught on the mast of an anchored spectator boat. The anchored boat was pulled on to her beam ends and the mizzen mast of the ketch snapped. Her crew swiftly cleared the mess away and consigned the broken rig to the deep. Strangely, *The Card*, as a sloop, became the overnight leader.

The fourth leg was to Punta del Este again and relatively uneventful all the way to Cape Horn. *Steinlager 2* went head-to-head with *Fisher & Paykel* all the way and approaching Cape Horn, after 19 days, had a lead of 20 miles while the two sloops, *Merit* and *Rothmans*, were more than 100 miles astern. Drizzle and light winds were the order of the day at the Cape for the leader which enabled Dalton to close right up to within five miles. The light winds continued into the Atlantic, allowing *Merit* and *Rothmans* to cut back the deficit by 40 miles.

With a 1,000 miles to go, the two leaders were within 100 metres of each other and the match race was on again. It continued all the way to Punta with '*Big Red*' finishing 22 minutes ahead in a strong tail wind. Behind them a drama was taking place. A radio message was heard from the Finnish Maxi, *Martela OF*; her navigator calling, 'Mayday, Mayday, our keel is falling off!'

Martela had suffered keel problems on the first leg and these had been rectified but recurred as the sloop made her way northwards from Cape Horn. Her crew had discovered the keel becoming lose but her skipper Markku Wiikeri decided to keep sailing because the wind was light. 'It felt safer to continue sailing,' he said, 'because the pressure on the keel stopped it moving.' When it finally went, the boat rolled over in 15 seconds.

Merit was 40 miles to the north and Alain Gabbay with *Charles Jourdan* was 40 miles to the west. Six and a half hours after both boats altered course to go to *Martela*'s aid the entire crew was aboard the other two competitors after being found safe and well sitting on the upturned hull. Both the rescuing boats received time allowances for diverting and going to the aid of the Finnish crew.

Rothmans was third home at first light, the morning after *Steinlager 2*'s finish. Her crew, to a man, marched straight up the sea wall at Punta to one of their favourite hang-outs – the Rat Hole. It may have been 0730, but the time didn't matter, they were thirsty and needed a drink. They stayed until they were sated.

It was not a good leg for the all-women crew of *Maiden* who finished a day and a half behind *L'Esprit de Liberté* and handed the French the lead in Class D.

The fifth leg saw *Rothmans*' navigator Vincent Geake take a course well to the east of the rest while the two New Zealand ketches and the rest of the fleet stayed closer to the Brazilian coast. *Rothmans* went into a 100 mile lead as they beat to windward. As they moved into the Doldrums however, *Rothmans* suffered the worst and it was not long before *Merit* and *Fisher & Paykel* had slipped through into the lead. *Steinlager 2* went with them and was soon back in her accustomed position.

The north-east Trades once again gave the ketches a distinct advantage and as they passed Barbuda, *Rothmans* was 110 miles behind the two leaders with *Merit* another 150 miles behind her. *Steinlager 2* held on to her lead over *Fisher & Paykel* to finish at Fort Lauderdale 34 minutes ahead with *Rothmans* another four hours behind. With *Merit* finishing 18 hours behind the leader, *Fisher & Paykel* went into second place overall for the first time in the race.

The final leg began with two rig failures which could have resulted in dismastings. On the first evening the Italian *Gatorade* (ex *NZI Enterprise*) reported a broken spreader and headed to Saint Augustine to effect repairs. The following day *Rothmans* had an intermediate shroud rod part. The crew was lucky to save the mast and headed for Georgetown to replace it. Their shore crew arrived in two Lear jets with a replacement rod and the turnaround time was just two hours, but by then *Rothmans* was 280 miles astern of the leaders.

On the fifth day at 0150 there was a loud crack aboard *Steinlager 2* as the port mizzen chainplate gave way. The big ketch was running with full sail set and initially the chainplate fabrication was still just holding to the deck. The mizzen spinnaker and the mizzen were dropped instantly and almost simultaneously there was another bang as the chainplate broke completely. Brad Butterworth swung the wheel and crash-gybed the boat so that the load came on the starboard side rigging. The situation had been doubly dangerous as the chainplate also took the load of the main running backstay and the race leader might easily have been sitting in the Atlantic without a mast to her name.

Two days later, *Satquote British Defender* was not so lucky. The topmast shroud failed and down came the top of her mast. Her race was virtually at an end, but skipper Colin Watkins organised a jury rig with all that he had available and sailed a less than fast passage back to Southampton, taking six-and-a half days longer than the leader.

Even *Fisher & Paykel* did not escape without a scary moment. Her mizzen forestay parted and she was lucky not to lose her aft mast for the second time. She was never very far from *Steinlager 2* and led for much of the way, but as on every leg, when push came to shove, it was *Steinlager 2* that went to the front when it most counted and the boat which led the fleet out of Hurst Narrows, was leading them back in.

Southampton Water was packed almost solid with craft as the leader made her way to the finish. The gun fired and the arms of all the Kiwis aboard *'Big Red'* were raised in triumph. Peter Blake had finally won the Whitbread Trophy. The crew waited for 36 minutes to cheer their fellow countrymen on *Fisher & Paykel* as they crossed the line. It was a resounding Kiwi victory; two entries – first and second.

2

Design Development

The birth of the Whitbread 60

W hen the race was conceived, the International Offshore Rule (IOR) was the authority in its sphere. It had been developed, by the request of all off-shore yachting nations, to handicap boats from 18 to more than 70 feet so that they might all, theoretically, race on a level basis. It was an idea with perhaps too much idealism in it – it was to be all things to all men.

But the highly sophisticated IOR was all there was and the Royal Naval Sailing Association was stuck with it. Boats were being built to that rule and, at the time, the worst tendencies had not been explored by designers and owners. By and large, the racing was seen to be close, at least in events of no more than 600 miles. There were some questions as to how it should be used, since the Rule itself only pro-vides a boat with a theoretical rating based on measurements of the hull and rig.

Somehow, those ratings have to be converted into a factor that will adjust the elapsed time of each boat proportionately. This can be calculated as a factor of time elapsed or of the distance sailed. The former was popular in Britain while North American sailors preferred the latter, knowing when they started the race, just how much time they allowed, or were allowed by each yacht in it. The RNSA decided that time on distance was the more equitable way for the long distance race and calculated time allowances accordingly.

The first race attracted a wide variety of craft. There were those, like Chay Blyth's *Great Britain II*, that were built specially for the race, and others as old as *Keyway-din*, built in 1913. In between there were boats of many different types including series production yachts. The world of ocean racing on the blue waters of the world was in its infancy. One thing was standard amongst them – by today's standards they were all of heavy displacement. This was common among almost every rac-ing boat in the early 1970s, but a revolution was about to occur which would have significant relevance to the boats which would take part in future Whitbreads.

The early races had a greater variety, too, in the type of sailing which might be expected. The leg from The Solent to Cape Town was one in which there was a great deal of windward sailing; this suited the heavier displacement boats better than the lighter ones which were to follow. The big change came with the fifth race in 1989/90 when the political climate in South Africa was considered incorrect for a Cape Town stopover and the course had to be redrawn dramatically.

The only way open to the organisers was to head first for Punta del Este, the third stopover port of the previous race, and then cross the Southern Ocean to Freman-tle, introduced as a new stopover because it was considered that going straight to Auckland would be too far. In doing so, the race organisers removed almost all the windward sailing from the race, further encouraging light displacement downwind flyers. The causes were all too readily apparent, as were the effects when a hardier breed of sailors, eager to achieve the similar sort of results they had scored over smaller race courses, attacked the Whitbread with a new fervour.

Yacht designers will often suggest ways of winning races by developing certain parameters within the rules of design, construction and rating of racing yachts, and they are always encouraged by sailors. It is the root of yacht design development and nowhere is the influence greater than in the Grand Prix areas, and the Whitbread rapidly became one of these. There was a demand, too, for greater public perception; explaining the intricacies of the IOR to the man-in-the-street is slightly more than simply difficult and he also wants the first to finish to be the winner. That did not occur, in any form, until the 1989/90 race when there was a Maxi class, although the overall winner was still determined by handicap.

As early as the 1981/82 race, the favoured light displacement designs had been adequately demonstrated to be efficient. Peter Blake's *Ceramco New Zealand*, a Farr designed 68 ft sloop, would undoubtedly have been the handicap winner but for a dismasting on the first leg. The writing (in favour of light displacement) was on the wall, but Blake, strangely, did a volte-face and changed both designer and concept for the following race, when Ron Holland produced the heaviest boat in the race for him. Pierre Fehlmann, in his third Whitbread, went to Farr, after seeing *Ceramco*'s performance, and his *UBS Switzerland* was the elapsed time winner. Farr, while continuing a light displacement theme, had suffered some of the constraints of the IOR, but *UBS* was lighter than the other Maxis in that year.

When the race became more of a downhill slide, in 1989 there was greater encouragement for designers to exploit the IOR to provide boats with better reaching and running performance. With a maximum IOR rating of 70 ft, designers took different attitudes to the way in which speed around the world might best be achieved; some heading further towards lighter displacement than others. The efficacy of the light displacement designs was adequately displayed by the performances of both Alain Gabbay's *Charles Jourdan* and Javier de la Gandara's *Fortuna Extra Lights*.

Charles Jourdan came from the board of Guy Ribadeau Dumas and was only 72 ft overall. Sailed with an 11 man crew, six less than was carried on *Fisher & Paykel*, *Charles Jourdan* finished sixth overall. *Fortuna Extra Lights* displayed some blisteringly fast speeds in the Southern Ocean and, in one 24 hour period, logged a record 403 miles, the first monohull to have broken the 400 barrier.

Heavy boats were to be found at the back of the pack and while it was known that the days of the IOR were extremely limited, there was nothing else remotely ready to become the 'Whitbread' rule. But while the fifth race was in progress, there were moves afoot to change all that.

What had changed, over the years, were the rigs of the competing boats. Two-masters were common in the first race, simply because the technology to build and rig sufficiently tall masts for Maxis did not exist. Conny van Rietschoten deliberately plumped for a ketch rig on his first *Flyer*, winner of the second race, and had asked for a similar rig for his Maxi for the next race. *Flyer II* shared the lofting and frame patterns of Herbert von Karajan's *Helisara* built at Huisman's yard and would have needed considerable expensive alteration to the structure of the hull so the idea was dropped. This was to be regretted by van Rietschoten, because, despite finishing first on every leg, all but two weeks of the race were spent reaching or running where the two-masted rig would have been at its most effective.

Technology improved and with it the height of masts increased and their diameters decreased. Less weight aloft meant better sail-carrying ability and the performance of the boats improved dramatically. But it was Bruce Farr who was responsible for the ultimate speed gains of the Maxi-raters when he returned to the ketch rig in 1989/90.

The technology of hull construction – the change from wood, steel and aluminium alloy, to high-tech reinforced plastics including carbon fibre in the hulls – allowed for greater sail-carrying capacity and the IOR rewarded the ketch rig (and also the schooner) disproportionately. Nothing could have been more obvious than the exploitation of the rule as far as rigs were concerned. Bruce Farr offered the ketch option to all four of his clients entered for the 1989/90 race and only Pierre Fehlmann decided against it.

The extra sail area appealed to those skippers who believed that speed was all about sail area and both Roger Nilson and Grant Dalton were early to commit themselves. By being the last of the ketch builders, Peter Blake was able to take the rig one step further in a fractional rig, the extra height of which gave him an edge of speed over the masthead boats in lighter airs. It was to prove valuable towards the end of most legs.

When the sixth race got under way, four years later, Farr and his clients had progressed the equation further, looking for every square centimetre of sail area that they could achieve. The heights of mizzen masts approached those of the mainmast – the race organisers had ruled against schooners – and all three of the new Maxis, from Farr, came out in this configuration. Lawrie Smith, faced with the uphill struggle of 'supercharging' *Fortuna*, after a huge design and development programme, went as far as he dared towards having more sail area on the mizzen rig than there was on the forward one. Regretably, development time was against him and the mizzen rig collapsed just one day into the race.

Throughout the six Whitbread races, it is not only the hulls and rigs which have altered, there has also been tremendous development in winches, deck gear and sail material. The race has, indeed, been a technical laboratory for the hardware manufacturers and, as a result, yachtsmen throughout the world have benefited from the developments which have orginated in this ocean marathon.

It was well understood that the days of the IOR were coming to a close, but there was nothing on the horizon good enough for the Whitbread. The International Measurement System (IMS) had begun as a cruiser/racer rule and was far from entering its grand prix stage when a suggestion was made to the Whitbread Organisers by the Offshore Maxi Yacht Association (OMYA) that a 60 ft one-design should be introduced as a second class to the Maxis. For the owners of the larger boats, this had a double-edged advantage in that it would produce new sailors who would want to move up from the 60 ft class and at the same time it would provide no threat to a dying class.

It did not, however, find universal support, many seeing it as a crutch for the dinosaur. The 60 footer was to be an IOR style boat, taking at least two days longer than the Maxis for each leg. This was regarded as a retrograde step in the eyes of many yachting *aficionados* and commentators worldwide. Time for change was running out and at a cocktail party, during the second stopover in Uruguay in March 1990, a small group was presented with an alternative suggestion. It was that Whitbread should fund a rule formulation project for a class for the next race. The proposal found some immediate interest and a detailed paper on the subject was provided so that the Whitbread Board might consider its viability. A meeting of skippers and others proposing to take part in the next race was called to discuss it at the next race stopover in Fort Lauderdale. The meeting was presented with a paper written by Rob Humphreys and Bob Fisher, giving the alternatives available, even to a major rethinking and reworking of the IOR so that, to use Humphreys' own words, 'we should not throw out the baby with the bathwater.' In reply, there were those who wanted a 'box' rule, one in which only the basic parameters would be defined; others wanted to adopt those few parameters as are used by the boats which race in the BOC Singlehanded Race. None quite seemed to understand what it was that the race organisers had in mind.

What was required was a rule which would give yacht designers some room for manoeuvre but at the same time, instantly produce a class in which the racing would be close in all weather conditions. The boats had to have some construction restrictions to make them less expensive, relatively, than the Maxis where all-out technological warfare had more than doubled the cost of a boat in the period between two races. The rule needed the input of the best brains in the world of yacht design and construction together with an element of sage rule writing to keep it in line with the other major international rules.

The new America's Cup class rule formulation had pointed to the way in which the operation might be successful and all the lessons learned from that operation - good and bad – were observed in setting up the organisation for the Whitbread 60 Rule. A three-day conference was convened at Goodwood, to which the leading racing yacht designers were invited, together with construction experts and a leavening of rule makers. It was co-ordinated by Fisher under the chairmanship of David Pritchard-Barrett, a two-man team which was to see the rule through to its publication.

The design conference was held at the beginning of June 1990 with a brief that the rule had to be available for presentation to competitors at a meeting held at the London Boat Show at the beginning of January 1991. It was a formidable project but the progress made at the three day conference put the entire operation into perspective and gave admirable direction to the group which was subsequently formed to process the deliberations.

The Whitbread Offshore Rule had to produce boats which were faster, safer, more exciting to sail and less expensive than their IOR counterparts. It was to be a totally new rule, one which did not intend to rate existing boats or provide the basis for handicaps; rather, to produce level rating yachts to the differing ideas of various designers. It had to be type forming so that the boats commissioned from a variety of designers, were all to be capable of sailing at very much the same speed.

The conference divided into groups to deal with various aspects of the rule – length measurement, rig, water ballast and construction. Perhaps the trickiest point was that of length. It is generally understood that the length of a boat is a controlling factor in its maximum hull speed. That 'length' is not overall or waterline but the 'sailing length' which includes part of its forward and aft overhangs. Therefore much of the effort of this group, under the leadership of David Pedrick, was devoted to defining this length. The forward and aft overhang components are calculated from the measurement of two forward and two aft girths and from these an intersection of the component lines with a defined waterplane establishes the 'sailing length,' L. In basic terms, more girth aft would require a reduced static waterline length, while the bow girths control the rake of the stem – this is also restricted to a maximum of 35° from the vertical.

It was decided that all measurements should be taken out of the water and then flotation marks be impressed in the hull. The boat is then floated and ballasted, if necessary, until she sits at those marks in measurement condition in a manner similar to that employed in the metre boat classes for many years. It is a system in which sailors have confidence. Since the only acceptable method of determining the displacement of a yacht is to weigh it, it was decided that modern loadcells accurate to within 50 kg in 20 tonnes could adequately provide the correct information and all boats built to the rule would therefore have to be weighed.

The rig is almost one-design with predetermined maximum heights of the mast and foretriangle. The base of the foretriangle also has a defined maximum measurement as are the spinnaker leech and bowsprit lengths. Every encouragement is given to rigs without overlapping headsails so that the shrouds can be taken to chainplates on the hull shell, rather than inboard, which provides a stronger staying base for the rig. Fully battened mainsails with girth controls to limit the roach were considered efficient; the limited roach is so that they will clear the mandatory standing backstay. Masthead spinnakers and drifters were very much part of the philosophy of the rule but the use of these sails was restricted by the RNSA in order to preserve the 'premium quality' of the Maxis. The rule was seen to have been capable of producing 60 footers which would effectively beat the 85 ft Maxis; and so it proved.

Water ballast was always considered as a viable speed producing factor to be encouraged. It is limited by tanks of no more than 5 000 litres capacity. Water is also the racing sailor's enemy and much thought was given to the safety of the Whitbread 60 class with a demand for the hull to be divided into at least four watertight compartments (excluding the tankage) by watertight bulkheads, two forward and one aft. There is, in the rule, a requirement for the minimum height of the deck above the water with any one of the compartments flooded.

All-in-all, the final rule meets all the policy requirements. It produces fast, sloop rigged monohulls of similar performance, suitable for long distance racing offshore at the highest level of the sport. The need for safety is paramount and the rule is intended to foster design developments leading to easily driven, seaworthy yachts of high stability, requiring moderate crew numbers.

Yachting columnist Andrew Preece described the impact of the rule as giving a new focus to the race. 'It has centred the attention away from the Maxis,' he said. 'It does remain to be seen,' he added, 'whether their racing will be close.' He believed that it would put the deciding factor of the race increasingly on the people rather than the boats which they sail. He felt that it is was a possibility that the 60s may beat the Maxis on certain legs but pointed to the performance of the light displacement boats in the 1989/90 race where they produced some prodigious daily runs but were unable to sustain high speeds over an entire leg. 'It will also depend on whether they (the Race Committee) slow them down any more.'

It was prophetic and heady stuff and has been shown, throughout this race, to be true. With masthead spinnakers on all of the legs, there is little doubt that the overall winner on elapsed time would have been a Whitbread 60.

3

What it takes to win the Whitbread Race
Preparation

Preparation pays. That lesson shone through even after the first stage of this latest Whitbread Round the World Race. Those with most sea miles under their keels did best while the disasters befell those who had put in minimal preparation. Take Lawrie Smith's Spanish Maxi *Fortuna* for instance. Stretched from 76 to 85 ft and fitted with a radical mizzen wing mast, her crew experienced little more than 25 knots of wind during their short practice trials in The Solent, and did not find out that their keel was too small until competing in their one pre-race competition, the Fastnet.

Then, 25 hours after leaving The Solent at the start of the Whitbread, *Fortuna's* mizzen mast tumbled down when her bumpkin collapsed under the strain. A few days later, after a 50 knot gale, her main mast followed, and in between, several of her titanium deck-bolts gave way, unable to cope with the sheet loadings.

At the front of the fleet, however, *New Zealand Endeavour* and *Tokio*, the two class leaders, suffered little in the way of damage – and nothing that could not be repaired onboard. Grant Dalton, skipper of *New Zealand Endeavour* was on his fourth Whitbread, and between them, his crew counted 17 circumnavigations. Before the race, they had spent six months training in European waters. 'That has been very expensive but it was very important for us to get as much competitive experience against our rivals as possible. Otherwise, you don't find out your own weaknesses until it is too late.' Dalton emphasised.

After tuning up in *New Zealand* waters, *New Zealand Endeavour* was shipped to Britain in time to compete in the UAP Round Europe race and finished first among the Maxis both in this race and the Fastnet. 'We learned a great deal from those events, and as a result, re-defined the boat's rating to improve her down wind speed,' says the skipper.

Fellow *New Zealand*ers Chris Dickson and Ross Field both chose to mount two-boat programmes. *Yamaha*, Field's second Bruce Farr design proved fastest on the first leg, winning the Omega 24 hour challenge with a run of 343.7 miles, but fell down tactically in the Doldrums and finished third in class.

Tokio by contrast led the fleet out of The Solent and finished first among the 60 footers just 3 hours 7 minutes behind *New Zealand Endeavour*. Skipper Chris Dickson said on arrival, 'We didn't encounter any conditions that we hadn't seen during our training.'

Before shipping his boat to England, Dickson and his crew spent 11 days down in the Southern Ocean during mid-winter to find out what it was like. 'It was damned cold – and windy,' he recalls. 'We had 45-55 knots of breeze for two days and it didn't go much below 40 knots for several days either side.

It was so bad, the veterans among *Tokio*'s crew who counted seven Whitbread races between them, agreed that they had never seen anything like it. 'We went down there saying that we didn't need this or that, and came back knowing that we did.' Dickson added.

During their early dip down into the Southern Ocean, Dickson and his crew also gained a timely lesson about the fragility of the Whitbread 60s when the boat suffered early delamination problems in the bows. That area of the boat was subsequently beefed up with the addition of more ring frames which cured the problem for good.

As for his two-boat programme, Dickson reiterated: 'There are things with a two-boat programme that you never learn with one boat. I've seen that happen too often in the America's Cup. When one boat is quicker, you work out why, then transfer that knowledge to the other boat.' Dickson, competing in his first Whitbread, covered more than 15,000 miles during the previous 12 months.'I learned a lot from competing aboard *Victoria*, a 70 ft sled in the 2,200 mile Transpac and when we raced both Whitbread boats in the Suva Race, we gained a lot from the light winds experienced,' he added.

Dennis Conner's *Winston* team, shelved plans to build a second boat, and racing against penniless back-markers like Nance Frank's *US Women's Challenge* and the British entry *Dolphin & Youth* learned little about their own boat in the 3000 mile Transatlantic Gold Cup race before the big event. By the time they had finished third in the Fastnet Race, Brad Butterworth and his team knew they would have their work cut out – and by then it was too late.

On the other hand, *Galicia '93 Pescanova* the Spanish 60 footer, skippered by Javier de la Gandara spent as much time as possible tuning up against her European rivals and went on to win the Fastnet and share honours in the Round Europe race with Roger Nilson's *Intrum Justitia*. As a result perhaps, the Spanish finished second to *Tokio* into Punta del Este.

Word leaked out to both *Intrum Justitia* and *Yamaha* camps about the potential delamination in the bows, and extra strengthening was added during construction. But others did not hear of the potential weakness and it cost them dearly. *Galicia*, for instance, though raced extensively in Northern Europe before the Whitbread, did not experience anything like the harsh conditions of the Southern Ocean, and dropped from second to sixth on the long second leg across the Indian Ocean when the crew had to shore up her blistering forefoot with a cut-down spinnaker pole, floorboards and pots and pans.

Winston suffered a similar fate on this leg, though the slamming to windward for 12 hours when Butterworth and his crew turned back into the cresting seas of the Southern Ocean for 12 hours in search of *Brooksfield*, may well have contributed to these problems.

Delamination was not a problem confined to the Whitbread 60s. Grant Dalton's Maxi *New Zealand Endeavour* also suffered a breakdown between the two skins and lightweight core sandwiched between them, and the boat underwent considerable surgery before the big event. The New Zealand winner suffered problems in the bow area again during five days of hard windward work during the fifth leg up the Brazilian coast, but it was nothing compared to the damage sustained to Eric Tabarly's hapless French challenger *La Poste*. When she arrived in Fort Lauderdale, the damage was so bad that one complete section of the hull had to be cut out, and a new man-sized section, moulded in France, was airfreighted out to be laminated in.

Grant Dalton learned all about preparation from that master of detail, Cornelis van Rietschoten when he crewed for the Dutchman aboard his 1981/82 Whitbread winner *Flyer*.

Van Rietschoten had set a standard that far exceeded his rivals in the previous race when his first *Flyer*, a 65 ft ketch-rigged S&S design won the first leg, beating much larger rivals boat for boat and went on to pick up the principal handicap trophy.

While others concentrated merely on getting their boats to the start line on time, Van Rietschoten covered more than 10 000 miles in *Flyer*, winning the Trans-atlantic Race that year before returning to Holland to make more than 100 modifications to the yacht. He put that first success down to 80 per cent preparation, 10 per cent tactics – and 10 percent luck, and proved it all again four years later with his second *Flyer*, a Frers designed Maxi, which not only won on elapsed time, but secured handicap honours as well.

Peter Blake, one of the most experienced ocean sailors, finally won the 1989/90 Whitbread at his fifth attempt. His Kiwi Maxi *Steinlager 2* won every leg, and reflected the lessons from 20 years of bitter disappointment. Even so, the whole carefully planned programme came perilously close to falling down when a chainplate supporting both masts suddenly gave way. Blake's race was saved only by the quick reactions of Brad Butterworth on the wheel who crash gybed the boat instinctively to save the rig.

Four years later, Chris Dickson was less fortunate. After building up a comfortable 14 hour lead over the fleet, his world came crashing down when *Tokio* was dismasted off the Brazilian coast. As a result, the team dropped from first to fifth in class. Dickson and his crew refused to speculate on what went wrong. 'By the time we had recovered all the bits back onboard, there was too much damage to pinpoint any one item,' one of his crew explained. Others, however, pointed to the pins holding the diagonal shrouds in place on the mast just below each spreader bracket, an acknowledged weak link within the Whitbread 60 rig. One failed on *Galicia* during the first leg though mercifully for Javier de la Gandara and his Spanish crew, it did not lead to a dismasting. 'After that, the mast makers faxed out a warning advising us to change all the pins after each leg,' said Lawrie Smith.

As the race has become more closely fought, crew ability has become a premium. In the days of van Rietschoten's victories, the principal requirements of any youngster signing on was that he be a pleasant, hard working individual who could keep his food down! Bluewater racing experience was a secondary requirement. Training and team building came with the job during 10 000 miles of pre-race transatlantic sailing.

Pierre Fehlmann used the same formula aboard his Maxi *UBS Switzerland* to win line honours in the 1985 race, but by 1993, the game had moved on and the young blood on *Merit Cup* was never a match for the experience of 17 circumnavigations within Dalton's *New Zealand Endeavour* crew.

The weather has always been another major factor dividing winners from losers. *Ocean Passages of the World,*'The British Admiralty tome published by the Hydrographer of the British Admiralty giving empirical data from the great days of sail, was the bible then, and it was only in 1981 that crews began to make a serious study of the weather patterns. Van Rietschoten commissioned the Weather Centre at Bracknell to produce an analysis culled from a century of records to provide a computerised 'guesstimate' as to how weather systems would develop during the race. The research was never fully completed, but in helping to compile the information,

Daniel Wloszcowski, *Flyer*'s French navigator, gained such a wealth of information that he became a Met buff in his own right.

The difference was significant and is best compared with *Flyer 1*'s performance in the 1977/78 race when the crew found themselves on the wrong side of low pressure systems more than a dozen times. Wloszcowski by contrast, mis-read the patterns only once – when Blake's *Ceramco NZ* gained a 40 mile lead after leaving New Zealand. As a result, *Flyer* sliced a massive 14 days off the race record, despite languishing in the Doldrums during the outward leg for six days!

Now, the role of navigator has changed to tactician, met man and computer buff rolled into one. Skippers can tell where they are at the press of a button. What they need to know is where they should be in a few days time to make the most from a changing weather pattern. This was one lesson Ross Field learned the hard way. Closing on the Doldrums during the first leg, his yacht, which had been running second just two miles behind *Tokio*, lost almost 200 miles after crossing through the wrong point on the Equator. He lost a similar amount again on the second stage across the Southern Ocean when caught out again by the weather. 'If there is a single factor that contributed to our win, it was replacing Godfrey Cray our navigator with a weather expert,' he admitted at the finish.

Cray, who had partnered Field on Blake's *Steinlager 2* four years ago, got off the boat in Fremantle to be replaced for one leg only by veteran Kiwi ocean racer Murray Ross. But Field's greatest break came when he selected Nik White, a professional meteorologist with little previous sailing experience, for the last three legs of this 32,000 mile race.

According to Field, White's analysis of how to play the fourth stage from Auckland around Cape Horn to Punta del Este proved unerringly accurate, though his team still had difficulty in putting the game plan into practice. They finished third within the Whitbread 60 class, five hours behind *Intrum Justitia* but more promisingly just eight minutes behind the then race leader *Tokio*.

Faith in White's expertise finally paid off in a big way on the fifth leg to Fort Lauderdale when *Yamaha* sailed around *Intrum* to pull off a massive 14 hour lead in the Doldrums. From that point on, it was merely a question of covering Smith's challenge on the final stage which Field and his crew did admirably right across the Atlantic.

Another to build a reputation for making the right weather calls in the 1993/94 race was Marcel van Triest, the Dutch navigator on *Intrum Justitia*. His greatest gamble was to call for a gybe south after rounding Prince Edward Island mid-way across the Indian Ocean. At the time, *Intrum Justitia* led the fleet but had *Tokio* just 15 minutes astern. 'Marcel was adamant we should go that way, but I have to admit to my doubts. I kept saying we were on the wrong gybe,' said Smith in Fremantle. While the rest of the fleet, continued trucking eastwards, *Intrum Justitia*'s southerly turn became increasingly isolated until a fresh gale sent the European entry scurrying into the record books with the first of several record 24 hour runs, to build an unassailable lead.

Van Triest's mastery of the complex weather patterns came into their own again on the fourth leg when he took *Intrum Justitia* down to 63 °S, 400 miles closer to the ice than their rivals.

This time round, the weather systems surrounding one of the world's bleakest headlands proved more complex than usual, leaving the Horn bathed unusually in balmy sunshine while seven low pressure systems following in quick succession of each other, battered the fleet 100 miles to the south. Both *Winston* and *Yamaha* took wrong turns which cost each of them almost half a day's run, but *Intrum Justitia's* weather guru picked his way through the climatic minefield with masterful intuition to lead the fleet round in record time. The weather lesson was also learned by *Winston* who shipped American routing expert Billy Biewenga (another veteran from *Flyer*) aboard for the last transatlantic dash and was rewarded with second place across the line.

Complex computer programmes, satellite pictures beamed directly to the yachts and weather forecasts broadcast to the fleet via each yacht's INMARSAT-C terminal helped to provide a better picture, but the lessons were clear. To get an edge, get a met man onboard!

So what does it take to win the Whitbread? A big budget certainly. No one has ever succeeded in this race with shoe-string finance. Back in 1978, victory cost the Dutch winner around £750,000. By 1982, the cost of campaigning a Maxi to win both line and handicap honours had risen to £1.25 million. Today, a Whitbread 60 costs £700,000 to build, £800,000 will go in wages for the crew and support team, £500,000 in sails, and a further £1 million will get gobbled up in maintenance and campaign costs. On top of this, the sponsor must add £1 million or more to take advantage of the publicity opportunities that a race like this affords, and another £1 million if a two-boat programme is envisaged.

The payback is three years of high level publicity worldwide, across a wide spectrum of the media from television to pages on sport, business and leisure.

As we have seen, the second vital ingredient is preparation. Last minute campaigns have never proved successful in this race, however much cash is thrown at trouble-shooting problems later. Time is needed to perfect a design and build a team good enough to win. There is no substitute either for distance under the keel to test both boat and crew. And as Chris Dickson proved, some of that testing time needs to be in the heavy conditions of the Southern Ocean or North Atlantic to shake out as many weak links as possible before the race.

And finally there is van Rietschoten's 10 percent luck value. In a race of this duration, luck has a habit of turning full circle. The question has more often been whether competitors are well enough prepared to take full advantage when the dice roll their way, and good enough to minimise the losses when luck turns against them. Lawrie Smith lost the 1993/4 race in the Doldrums, but the 150 miles that *Yamaha* pulled out while *Intrum Justitia* was becalmed might well have been compensated for had this European crew finished better than fifth on the first leg to Punta del Este.

'Some people just don't have lucky fingers, but like Arnold Palmer's famous quote – 'The more I practice, the luckier I seem to become,' says Cornelis van Rietschoten. He points to Peter Blake as a typical example. 'It took him five attempts at the Whitbread during which he experienced every set-back from near sinking to dismasting before everything went right,' he says recalling *Steinlager 2's* clean sweep of the silverware in the 1989/90 race.

4

Race preview

The 16 yachts and their skippers

Six IOR Maxi yachts and ten water-ballasted light displacement designs built to the new Whitbread 60 ft rule entered for the sixth running of this classic global marathon.

Starting from Southampton, England on 25 September, the course took in Punta del Este, Uruguay; Fremantle, Australia and Auckland, New Zealand before returning around Cape Horn to Southampton via Punta del Este and Fort Lauderdale. The one change to the course from four years before was the addition of Prince Edward Island in the Indian Ocean to keep the yachts from straying too far into the icy seas of the Southern Ocean.

Long before the start, the race was seen as a swan-song for the IOR Maxi class, but nevertheless, three $5 million Bruce Farr design ketches were built specifically for the event, and another, the converted Spanish ketch *Fortuna* was made unrecognisable from her days as a sloop rigged mini-Maxi. She was seen as the dark-horse in this event, for this yacht, skippered by Lawrie Smith, carried almost 100 sq m more sail area than any of her rivals.

Fortuna's re-entry into racing was hardly impressive, finishing last among the Whitbread Maxis in the Fastnet Race. There was time to make further modifications, but not enough to pacify critics, particularly in Spain who, resenting Smith's appointment over a Spanish skipper, were quick to label the boat a dog.

But Smith's problems did not end there. A week before the start, Richard Gibson, his Irish cook who had sailed the last race aboard *NCB Ireland*, was forced to withdraw with medical problems and Andrew Nash, a Zimbabwean chef, was plucked as a last minute replacement from one of the best eating houses in Lymington. Having sailed on a boat only twice before, no one knew if he would be seasick or not.

Then, to cap it all, 24 hours before the start, Russell Pickthall, *Fortuna*'s experienced sailmaker embarking on his third circumnavigation, was struck down with bronchial pneumonia. He joined the yacht against doctor's advice, moments before the Maxi left the dockside at Ocean Village and was prone in his bunk when the start gun fired. As Smith said prophetically over the radio, 'This is not a promising start'.

Another veteran from the 1989/90 race was *Uruguay Natural*, the former Finnish entry *Martela*, which lost its keel and capsized off Argentina during the last race. The hull was salvaged and, sponsored by the Uruguayan Tourist Agency; she won the 1993 Buenos Aires/Rio race.

Pre-race favourite was the Bruce Farr designed ketch *New Zealand Endeavour* skippered by Grant Dalton, a veteran from *Flyer*, Cornelis van Rietschoten's Dutch winner in 1981. He came close to victory again in the last race when his earlier yacht *Fisher & Paykel* finished second to *Steinlager 2* . This time, he had two identical Farr designs to contend with in the form of Pierre Fehlmann's Swiss Maxi *Merit Cup*, and *La Poste* skippered by the former postmaster, Daniel Mallé.

Four years before, the arguments had been about ketch versus sloop rigs. This time they centred on the distinctive clipper bow profile of the Bruce Farr designs. British measurers ruled that they should incur a rating penalty, a point hotly contested by other measurers in France and New Zealand. Ken Weller, the Offshore Racing Council's chief measurer, called in for an interpretation, took six months to decide the issue, and never did get round to ruling officially whether *Fortuna* could have a similar beak profile. The delay was inexcusable and led directly to a slanging match between Dalton and *Fortuna* skipper Lawrie Smith. 'It's a shame that the sport has to endure people like Smith,' said Dalton 'whose idea of fair play and sportsmanship seems to be distorted. Smith's antics have been no more than a misguided attempt at a smoke screen and he would serve his sponsors and country better by concentrating more on the job of winning on the water, rather than trying to drag the sport and the Whitbread race into a non-issue technical argument.'

Dalton concluded, 'The end result of all this is that Smith has made a number of misinformed allegations which have sadly discredited both himself, the Whitbread race and the sport from which he derives his income.'

All strong stuff – and much more was said off the record before the two ever got round to locking horns on the water.

Within the Whitbread 60 class, money was equally divided between *Winston*, Dennis Conner's well funded entry, and the two Japanese/New Zealand entries *Yamaha* and *Tokio*. The America's Cup maestro left it almost to the last moment to decide which (if any) legs he would sail, having placed Brad Butterworth, a veteran watch leader from Peter Blake's *Steinlager 2* entry, to lead the campaign.

Ross Field who headed the rival *Yamaha* group, was also a *Steinlager 2* watchleader and led the first Whitbread entry to mount a two-boat campaign. His first Bruce Farr design was chartered to America's Nance Frank who found a private backer in fellow crew Susie Chiu to fund preparations for her *US Women's Challenge* but struggled right up to the day of the start to find sponsorship to actually compete in the race.

Like Conner, Chris Dickson, the former New Zealand and Japanese America's Cup skipper, had not competed before in a trans-ocean, let alone trans-global event before this year (Conner did compete in the Transatlantic Race that year, which *Winston* won). However, funded by a Japanese advertising agency, he followed in Field's wake by mounting a two-boat campaign and surrounded himself with Whitbread veterans.

Dickson, dubbed 'the angry young man of yachting' by some, clashed with the race organisers almost immediately after the yachts had gathered in Ocean Village a week before the start. He believed that he had found a loop-hole in the tightly controlled sail plan rules governing the new Whitbread class, by developing a cross between a spinnaker and genoa for close reaching in all but the strongest of winds. Scrutineers questioned this novel 'gennaker' and it was promptly banned. Dickson was understandably upset.

'Effectively, *Tokio* has a loose-luffed genoa which they asked us to measure as a spinnaker,' said race director Ian Bailey-Willmot after seeing the sail in action. The sail was almost twice the size of standard headsails which, under the Whitbread 60 rules, are not allowed to overlap the mast. According to her crew, it could be set as close as 28° to the apparent wind. To meet the minimum width specification of a spinnaker, the aft one third of the sail had been made from a porous transparent film which curls in towards the mainsail without adversely affecting the airflow.

The international jury headed by Marcel Leeman, questioned the decision taken by the Whitbread 60 Council to ban the development, but could find no grounds to change the decision. Instead, they called on the Council to define what is, and is not, porous as far as cloth types are concerned.

The decision brought a sigh of relief among the other W-60 camps. 'It's a sensible decision' said one rival crewman. 'If it had been allowed, it would have started an arms race that the Whitbread 60 rule was brought in to avoid.' A crewman from *Winston* agreed. 'It would have been OK for us. We could have made up these sails overnight, but poorer syndicates like Matthew Humphries' *Dolphin & Youth* and the *US Women's Challenge* could not afford them and would start at even more of a disadvantage.'

Nance Frank, who led the penniless *US Women's Challenge*, had more pressing matters on hand to care too much about loop-holes in any sailing rules. She even had to miss the final skippers' briefing and photo call on the eve of the race in a desperate bid to head off the threatened seizure of her yacht. Frank made the start line of this race, only because bankers had worked through the night to save her challenge from sinking in a sea of unpaid bills. Four years ago, she had been forced by the same lack of cash to pull out of the race as soon as she crossed the start line – and it was those same debts that returned to haunt her again. She and her crew managed to make the start line – just, but the sails on their chartered yacht, many of which had well passed their sell-by date, failed to take the strain for long. Four large rips in as many days forced the crew to re-form into a sewing circle and spend 20 hours a day patching the remnants for much of the first unhappy leg.

The sole Russian entry in this race that began with the unlikely name of *Assol* under the stewardship of the equally unbelievable name of one, Vladimir Bugrov, failed to make the start after running out of money and US/Ukrainian entry *Odessa* skippered by Anatoly Verba arrived from Florida three days after the fleet had left Southampton. Her crew finally set sail seven days behind the rest after securing some second-hand sails left by *Brooksfield* and last minute sponsorship from the *Moscow Times* newspaper.

MAXI CLASS

Name: *Fortuna*
Country: Spain
Skipper: Lawrie Smith (UK)
Crew No: 15-17
Designer: Javier Visiers
Length overall: 24.8 m
Beam: 5.83 m
Displacement: 30,140 kg
Builder: Mefasa/Vision Yachts
Construction: Carbon/Kevlar/Nomex
Launch date: 1989 (Modified 1993)
Rig: Ketch
Sail area: 890 sq m
Ladbrokes Whitbread odds: 7:2

Fortuna was very much the dark horse within the fleet. The former ultra-light, which set a record 24 hour run of 403 miles during the 1989/90 race, was cut in half, extended by 2 metres and transformed into the heaviest displacement yacht in the fleet. She also carried the most sail area – up to 80 sq m more than *New Zealand Endeavour* on a giant glassfibre mizzen wing mast. British skipper Lawrie Smith was called in to lead the campaign after the converted yacht (without her oversized rig and new foils) did badly in the 1992 Route of Discovery Transatlantic Race. Under Smith's direction, the modified design underwent considerable tank and wind tunnel testing, but was not tested against her rivals until the Fastnet Race in August. Smith brought seven of his former *Rothmans* crew into the project, including Australian Shag Morton and Paul Standbridge as watch leaders. The crew also included Guillermo Altadill, their Tornado representative at the 1988 Olympics who coached Spain's four gold medal winning sailing team at Barcelona. He had sailed on *Fortuna* last time round and was the current Spanish Tornado champion. With him came Marc-Anton Corominas and Jesus Serrano, two young Spaniards who had been sailing on *Fortuna* for the past year. Last among his core team was Henri Hiddes the highly experienced South African based Dutchman who joined *Rothmans* from *NBC Ireland* four years before and was expected to strengthen the *Fortuna* team during the Southern Ocean legs.

Name: *La Poste*
Country: France
Skipper: Daniel Mallé (later replaced by Eric Tabarly)
Crew No: 16-18
Designer: Bruce Farr
Length overall: 25.9 m
Beam: 5.85 m
Displacement: 29,500 kg
Builder: Decision/Beneteau
Construction: Carbon/Kevlar/Nomex
Launch date: 1993
Rig: Ketch
Sail area: 830 sq m.
Ladbrokes Whitbread odds: 9:2

La Poste represented the French Post Office's second foray into the Whitbread race. In 1989, Mallé, a former postmaster from Lyons, sailed the Beneteau 51, the smallest boat in the fleet. Though ribbed about being the *'Last Post'* for always trailing the fleet, he and his crew of postal workers won considerable admiration for their cheerful delivery. Indeed, the project was such a success that the French postal service decided to enter again, this time with a competitive boat – a Bruce Farr designed sistership to Pierre Fehlmann's *Merit Cup*. The two yachts, which came off the same mould, were completed by Beneteau and the crews spent the early part of the season tuning and training together. This time round however, only half of Mallé's crew originated from within the postal service, the remainder being America's Cup, Olympic or Whitbread veterans. 'I have taken some like Benoit Caignaert, my second in command who comes from offshore racing and the America's Cup. There are also those who know the Southern Ocean like Joao Cabeçadas, who navigated for Patrick Tabarly,' explained Mallé. Other key recruits included Michel

Desjoyeaux the 1992 Figaro winner, and navigator Dominique Conin. By Fremantle however, the boat had proved consistently slower than *New Zealand Endeavour*
and *Merit Cup* so Mallé agreed to step down a rank in favour of French legend Eric
Tabarly who brought with him five of his top disciples to strengthen the team.

Name: *Merit Cup*
Country: Switzerland
Skipper: Pierre Fehlmann
Crew No: 16-18
Designer: Bruce Farr
Length overall: 25.9 m
Beam: 5.85 m
Displacement: 29,500 kg
Builder: Decision/Beneteau
Construction: Carbon/Kevlar/Nomex
Launch date: 1993
Rig: Ketch
Sail area: 830 sq m.
Ladbrokes Whitbread odds: 2:1

This was to be Pierre Fehlmann's fifth and last Whitbread campaign which he hoped
would emulate his 1985/86 entry *UBS Switzerland* which won overall line honours.
He returned four years later but his sloop rigged *Merit* was beaten into, third place
by the two New Zealand ketches, *Steinlager 2* and *Fisher & Paykel*.

Bringing Swiss precision to his preparations, Fehlmann shared all-important tank
and wind tunnel testing as well as training with the *La Poste* syndicate. He is a man
who prefers to train a new crew each time rather than fill the boat with 'rock-stars'
moulding them around a trusted afterguard who know how he likes things done.
That team of 'trusties' included Gerard Rogivue, Nicolas Berthaud, Andre Loepfe
and George Wagner.

Name: *New Zealand Endeavour*
Country: New Zealand
Skipper: Grant Dalton
Crew No: 16-18
Designer: Bruce Farr
Length overall: 26 m
Beam: 5.4 m
Displacement: 30,000 kg
Builder: Marten Marine
Construction: Carbon/Kevlar/Nomex
Launch date: 1992
Rig: Ketch
Sail area: 790 sq m
Ladbrokes Whitbread odds: 6:4 (favourite)

After spending the last race in the shadow of Peter Blake's *Steinlager 2* , Dalton exhibited the greatest commitment to winning this time round. Having gained support from seven New Zealand sponsors, he invested upwards of $50,000 on tank testing to gauge whether the new Whitbread 60s would beat the Maxi round the world. The Maxi won by 100 hours.

His Bruce Farr design was the first of the new breed to be launched in November '92 and for her opening debut, won line honours in the 630 mile Sydney to Hobart Race. Having been beaten last time by a heavier yacht carrying more sail area, some found it surprising that his boat design would again be between 50 - 100 sq m down on the quoted area of his principal rivals. This shortfall, however, appeared to make little difference in the light airs experienced during much of the UAP Round Europe Race which she won.

The four-time Whitbread circumnavigator surrounded himself with a deep pool of experience including Kevin Shoebridge, Glen Sowry. Alan Prior, Tony Rae, Craig Watson, and Cole Sheehan, together with Mike Quilter, Blake's former navigator.

Name: *Uruguay Natural*
Country: Uruguay
Skipper: Gustavo Vanzini Pons
Crew No: 16
Designer: German Frers
Length overall: 24.6 m
Beam: 5.92 m
Displacement: 29,200 kg
Builder: Baltic Yachts
Construction: Carbon/Kevlar/Nomex
Launch date: 1989
Rig: Fractional sloop
Sail area: 600 sq m
Ladbrokes Whitbread odds: 25:1

Uruguay Natural was the former *Martela OF* which lost her keel and capsized in spectacular fashion off Argentina during the fourth leg of the 1989/90 race. Her Finnish crew was rescued by Pierre Fehlmann's *Merit* and *Charles Jourdan* skippered by Alain Gabbay. The Frers design was salvaged and towed to Montevideo before being shipped back to Finland to be repaired.

Back in Uruguyan hands, her largely naval crew won the 1993 Buenos Aires/Rio race. She was never expected to be a match for the ketch-rigged yachts and was entered principally to give Gustavo Vanzini and his team valuable experience for future races.

WHITBREAD 60 CLASS

Name: *Brooksfield*
Country: Italy
Skipper: Guido Maisto
Crew No: 10
Designer: Bouvet/Petit
Length overall: 19.19 m
Beam: 5.2 m
Displacement: 13,500 kg
Builder: Tencara
Construction: Kevlar/foam sandwich
Launch date: 1992
Rig: Fractional sloop
Sail area: 417 sq m.
Ladbrokes Whitbread odds: 33:1

Brooksfield was drawn by the French team of Bouvet and Petit, two of the most experienced designers in water ballasted yachts, having shaped both Titouan Lamazou's 1990 Globe Challenge winner, *Ecureuil d'Aquitaine* and the second placed *Lada Poch*. However, early problems with *Brooksfield*'s keel led the two designers to call in fellow Frenchman Bertrand de Broc mid-way through the Globe Challenge solo round the world race when they were worried that similar keel fixings on his boat might also fail.

After a disappointing performance in the Route of Discovery Race, the boat was also sluggish in light airs during the UAP Round Europe warm-up to the Whitbread. But skipper Guido Maisto was a veteran from Georgio Falk's *Gatorade*, from where he gathered his key team-mates. One of the most experienced was Mauro Pelaschier, the former America's Cup skipper who had responsibility for tuning and speed, but after disagreements set in, he left the boat at Fremantle. Other *Gatorade* veterans included navigator Jan Herve, Richard Brisius and Andrea Proto.

Name: *Dolphin & Youth Challenge (later Reebok)*
Country: UK
Skipper: Matthew Humphries
Crew No: 12
Designer: Rob Humphreys
Length overall: 20.9 m
Beam: 5.25 m
Displacement: 13,500 kg
Builder: Vision Yachts
Construction: Kevlar/foam sandwich
Launch date: 1992
Rig: Fractional sloop
Sail area: 417 sq m
Ladbrokes Whitbread odds: 25:1

At 22, Matthew Humphries was the youngest skipper in the race. A crewmate aboard *With Integrity* (ex *Great Britain II*) the previous time round, he had wanted to race on *Rothmans* but was judged too young. Recent offshore successes belied his age however, for Humphries led his *Youth Challenge* to class victory in the 1991 Fastnet and Round Europe Race, and they finished a creditable third in the 1992 Round Britain Race.

Early in 1993, he and his crew combined their Whitbread aspirations with those of the Dolphin Challenge for disabled yachtsmen then led by James Hatfield in an effort to widen their appeal to sponsors. Hatfield walked out of the project midway through a press conference, leaving Humphries to take the wheel.

The first competitive outing for this combined disabled/youth crew was the Transatlantic Race in July where they gave Dennis Conner's *Winston* a run for her money in heavy airs, but fell back in the lighter going. Their Rob Humphreys designed yacht was paid for with a grant from the British based charity, Foundation for Sport and the Arts, and Reebok, which began as a part sponsor, and took up the name for the last leg from Fort Lauderdale.

Name: *Galicia '93 Pescanova*
Country: Spain
Skipper: Javier de la Gandara
Crew No: 10
Designer: Bruce Farr
Length overall: 19.75 m
Beam: 5.25 m
Displacement: 13,500 kg
Builder: Armada
Construction: Kevlar/foam sandwich
Launch date: 1993
Rig: Fractional sloop
Sail area: 417 sq m
Ladbrokes Whitbread odds: 6:1

This was Javier de la Gandara's second Whitbread race. He had been skipper of *Fortuna* for two legs during the last race when the Spanish sloop set a noon-to-noon record of 398 miles and exceeded 400 miles during a 24 hour period. His Bruce Farr design was sponsored by Galicia, the north-west coastal area of Spain where Gandara drew his crew. They were first to finish in the Fastnet Race, but later during scrutineering, it was found that her ballast tanks were larger than the rules allowed and they were hurriedly modified.

Name: *Hetman Sahaidachny*
Country: Ukraine
Skipper: Eugene Platon
Crew No: 10
Designer: Bruce Farr
Length overall: 19.45 m
Beam: 5.25 m
Displacement: 13,500 kg
Builder: Kajac/Katran/Viten

Construction: Kevlar/foam sandwich
Launch date: 1993
Rig: Fractional sloop
Sail area: 417 sq m
Ladbrokes Whitbread odds: 50:1

Eugene Platon was a veteran from *Fazisi*. Undaunted by that wet experience, he returned to the Ukraine in 1991 to lead his own project and promote his country's newly found independence on the world stage.

His Bruce Farr design was built at Kharkov in a former aerospace factory and his crew included *Fazisi* veterans Volodymyr Musatov and Yuri Doroshenko, together with former Olympic yachtsman Yuri Tokovoi and Soling champion Sergei Pichugin.

Name: *Intrum Justitia*
Country: Europe
Skipper: Roger Nilson (leg 1) Lawrie Smith (legs 2-6)
Crew No: 11
Designer: Bruce Farr
Length overall: 20 m
Beam: 5.25 m
Displacement: 13,500 kg
Builder: Green Marine
Construction: Kevlar/foam sandwich
Launch date: 1993
Rig: Fractional sloop
Sail area: 417 sq m.
Ladbrokes Whitbreads odds: 4:1

Roger Nilson first came to prominence as the doctor aboard Simon Le Bon's 1985/86 entry *Drum*. He campaigned *The Card* under Swedish colours in the 1989/90 event and returned this time with the European entered *Intrum Justitia* sponsored by one of Europe's largest debt collection agencies.

His crew were also pan-European and included Dutch navigator Marcel van Triest, Swedish America's Cup skipper Gunnar Krantz and Pierre Mas, skipper of the French Admiral's Cup yacht *Corum Saphir*. Nilson injured his knee at the finish of a disappointing first leg, and after flying home for surgery, was forced to retire from the race, handing over the project to Lawrie Smith.

Name: *Odessa*
Country: Ukraine/USA
Skipper: Anatoly Verba
Crew No: 10
Designer: Igor Sidenko
Length overall: 19.6 m
Beam: 5.25 m
Displacement: 14,200 kg

Builder: Volga Buran
Construction: Glassfibre/foam sandwich
Launch date: 1993
Rig: Fractional sloop
Sail area: 417 sq m
Ladbrokes Whitbread odds: 50:1

Another to be born from the *Fazisi* experience, *Odessa* led by Anatoly Verba was a joint Ukrainian/US campaign. The boat had been designed by Igor Sidenko, a consultant to the abortive 1992 Red Star America's Cup campaign and was built by the makers of the Soviet space shuttle. The half completed hull was then shipped to Tampa, Florida for completion. His crew was multi-national and included several adventurers who joined or left the crew at each port.

Name: *Tokio*
Country: Japan/New Zealand
Skipper: Chris Dickson
Crew No: 11
Designer: Bruce Farr
Length overall: 20 m
Beam: 5.25 m
Displacement: 13,500 kg
Builder: Cookson (Farr)
Construction: Kevlar/foam sandwich
Launch date: 1993
Rig: Fractional sloop
Sail area: 417sq m
Ladbrokes Whitbread odds 4:1

Chris Dickson chose different designers to produce rival boats for his challenge, then tested the two side by side, first to work them up America's Cup style before deciding which to race in the Whitbread. Bruce Farr and John Swarbrick designs were like chalk and cheese – the first conventional, while the second, drawn by Iain Murray's former design partner, boasted a wide stern, sharp nose and radical keel. The original 'Z' shaped foil was later replaced by a less complex foil with a lower wetted area, but in the end Dickson chose the more conventional Farr design to sail round the world. The America's Cup skipper picked Australian Andrew Cape as his navigator/tactician, together with American Mark Rudiger and Japan's Ken Hara to form a core crew which also included Whitbread veterans Barry McKay (who left prior to the race starting) and Matthew Smith.

Name: *US Women's Challenge* (previously *Yamaha 1* – renamed *Heineken* after leg 2)
Country: USA
Skipper: Nance Frank (replaced by Dawn Riley after Leg 1,
Crew No: 12
Designer: Bruce Farr
Length overall: 20 m
Beam: 5.25 m
Displacement: 13,500 kg
Builder: Cookson
Construction: Kevlar/foam sandwich
Launch date: 1992
Rig: Fractional sloop
Sail area: 417 sq m
Ladbrokes Whitbread odds: 16:1

No-one could fault Nance Frank's dedication to a cause. The American had hoped to compete against Tracy Edwards' *Maiden* crew to lead the first all-women crew to finish a Whitbread race, but lack of sponsorship limited her to making only a token start in the 1989/90 race.

Back again for the 1993 race, after seven years of banging the drum, she arrived back at Southampton without a sponsor but with private backing from crew-mate Susie Chiu to campaign Ross Field's discarded *Yamaha*, the prototype Bruce Farr 60 ft design. She competed in the New York to Southampton race and her crew included *Maiden* veterans Amanda Swan, fellow New Zealander Leah Newbold and Mikaela von Koskull from Finland. Three days before the start of the Whitbread it seemed history might repeat itself when creditors from Frank's previous campaign threatened to seize the boat if they were not paid. It took bankers until 0200 on the day of the start to agree that she could compete.

Name: *Winston*
Country: USA
Skipper: Dennis Conner/Brad Butterworth (NZ)
Crew No: 10/11
Designer: Bruce Farr
Length overall: 20 m
Beam: 5.25 m
Displacement: 13,500 kg
Builder: CCYD
Construction: Kevlar/foam sandwich
Launch date: 1993
Rig: Fractional sloop
Sail area: 417 sq m
Ladbrokes Whitbread odds: 5:2 (joint favourite)

Dennis Conner proved to be the master pragmatist when he announced his first challenge for the Whitbread. At an infamous press conference in San Diego after the equally infamous America's Cup in 1988, he had called Bruce Farr, who was the designer of his Whitbread race boat, 'You're nothing but a loser'.

Brad Butterworth, the man he chose to lead this campaign had also been on the wrong side of another famous Conner jibe when navigator to Chris Dickson's New Zealand Cup challenger in 1987. Then, the American had questioned 'Why else would you want to build a glassfibre boat unless you wanted to cheat?'

All this was buried in the interests of winning the longest race on record, in which their yacht *Winston* began as one of the pre-race favourites. The project attracted a strong team that included Irishman Gordon Maguire, Matteo Plazzi and Bouwe Bekking in the afterguard together with Frenchman Alexis Hellouin de Cenival and New Zealanders Dean Phipps, Peter Vitali, Dave Hurley, Mark Christiansen and Matthew Mason.

Name: *Yamaha*
Country: Japan/New Zealand
Skipper: Ross Field (NZ)
Crew No: 12
Designer: Bruce Farr
Length overall: 20 m
Beam: 5.25 m
Displacement: 13,500 kg
Builder: Cookson
Construction: Kevlar/foam sandwich
Launch date: 1993
Rig: Fractional sloop
Sail area: 417 sq m
Ladbrokes Whitbread odds: 5:2 (joint favourite)

Ross Field was the pace-setter in the Whitbread 60 class. Not only was he first to announce sponsorship, but also the first to launch a boat and the first in the 20 year history of the event to mount a two-boat campaign. The first *Yamaha* was launched in April 1992 and impressed everyone at the Kenwood Cup, before being dismasted during the delivery trip back across the Pacific to Japan. Boat No 2, also a Bruce Farr design was completed 12 months after the first and showed small but significant differences in shape, layout and keel configuration to her rivals.

Field, who had been a watch-leader on *Steinlager 2*, surrounded himself with other Whitbread veterans including Godfrey Cray, Jeff Scott, Robbie Naismith, Steve Trevurza and Joey Allen. Steve Cotton, Richard Bouzaid, Mark Hauser and Kazunori Komatsu from Japan completed the crew.

5

LEG ONE *Southampton to Punta del Este*

Tokio sets the pace

Despite the weather it was a exhilarating start to the sixth Whitbread race. The competing boats charged at the line as the starting gun was fired by the Duke of York aboard the Type 42 destroyer, *HMS Southampton*, and were immediately sailing at over 10 knots as they made their way towards the Forts in Spithead. The talking and the boasting were over, the race was on and the beginning of the truth would soon emerge.

The start was off Lee-on-Solent and there was a swept channel for the 14 competitors on a grey September afternoon with a 12-14 knot nor-westerly blowing. Spinnakers blossomed as the gun boomed out across the Eastern Solent and were soon pulling the boats as they carved white wakes into the grey waters. Those waters were not grey for long as the huge spectator fleet, estimated at more than 3,000 boats of varying sizes, from the giant cross-Channel ferries to ten foot rubber dinghies, churned it into white lumpy seas as they sped off in pursuit of the racing yachts.

To everyone's delight, the long awaited battle between the two former America's Cup antagonists, Chris Dickson and Dennis Conner, began the moment the starting signal had been made. Their two Whitbread 60s, *Tokio* and *Winston* were at the forefront of the fleet and battling for the honour to be first to Spithead and the Heineken buoy. Conner had opted for the southern, leeward end of the line, to leeward even of Lawrie Smith in *Fortuna*, with Dickson to windward of them both, but all were well clear of the bunch which developed close under *HMS Southampton* at the windward end of the line.

Winston's spinnaker was the first to go up, followed a second later by *Tokio*'s; both skippers choosing fractional asymmetrics. *Tokio*'s was the first to fill and the effect on the joint New Zealand/Japanese boat was dramatic. She almost leapt out of the water as the power of the filling sail hit the rig; *Tokio* was off – Dickson was seen to smile, albeit briefly – and the rest followed in her wake.

Conner was a length behind as his gennaker filled, the boat heeled steeply – the water ballast was not in the port side tank, Dickson's was, and the gap between them grew perceptibly until *Winston*'s tanks were full as well. It was a forceful demonstration of the extra power these craft develop when they have a 'bellyful' of water. Dickson and Conner had chosen the right end of the line and the two were soon well clear of the fleet, with Conner chasing and oblivious of the rest. As well he might, there were 31,975 miles to go.

At the windward end of the line, it was Daniel Mallé who claimed the front rank on the grid; he might even have beaten Dickson and Conner across, but *La Poste* did not have much way on because of the lee of the warship. As the two Whitbread 60s sped into the lead, the group of Maxis were slower to reach their top speed, but the dicing between them was every bit as fascinating.

La Poste set a spinnaker as did Pierre Fehlmann, a couple of boat lengths astern. But within half a mile of the start, Grant Dalton, the pre-race favourite with *New Zealand Endeavour*, set a number one jib top, pointed his boat higher than the other two and slipped through in the gap between them and sailed on to the weather hip of *La Poste*. *New Zealand Endeavour* continued to surge until her sails blanketed those of *La Poste*, whose spinnaker momentarily collapsed. She went through into the lead of the boats on the northern edge of the swept corridor, making the spectator boats scatter before her; risky perhaps, in view of what happened to the mizzen of *The Card* at the restart in Auckland in the previous race, but definitely spectacular.

Out in the middle, Matt Humphries steered the lone British entry, *Dolphin & Youth*, into third place. Having received a £200,000 boost to their funds through a last minute sponsorship deal with Reebok, the *Dolphin* crew were fired up to show the home crowd just how they could perform. They had to suffer a great deal of disturbed wash from the spectator craft and because of this, the lighter boat looked in danger of being 'rolled' by the heavier Maxis to windward when they decided to bear off for the Heineken buoy between the forts.

The breeze increased by a knot or two and the speedometers on *Tokio* and *Winston* began to flicker between 12 and 14 knots. Showing better speed than she had in the Fastnet Race six weeks earlier was Lawrie Smith's *Fortuna*; the change of keel appeared to stop her slipping sideways and the distinctive rig no longer looked ungainly.

Yamaha had been to leeward of the other Maxis, but the blue-hulled boat began to thread her way through the traffic and challenge them to windward just before they all gybed and made their way towards Bembridge Ledge buoy. By then, *Yamaha* was ahead of the Maxi pack although in danger of being buried by them.

Brooksfield seemed slow out of the blocks but with Italian America's Cup skipper Mauro Pelaschier at the wheel and a call for a masthead gennaker from skipper, Guido Maisto, the green hulled boat was soon up to challenge the bunch accompanied by Javier de la Gandara in the Fastnet Race winner, *Galicia '93 Pescanova*. Watching her from one of the *Winston* support boats was Francois Pino, the crewman who lost his left hand in an accident on board shortly before the Fastnet.

Roger Nilson's *Intrum Justitia* was late off the line, having to take the bad air from the group of boats bunched at the weather end and also having to accept the big lee given by the starting warship. Soon, however, her spinnaker, with the sponsor's slogan 'Fair Pay' emblazoned across it, began to be in evidence and the gap between her and the boats in front began to diminish.

Nance Frank and the *US Women's Challenge* were slow to start due to difficulties engaging a main halyard lock. They took their time to sort out the problem and settled into their stride before hoisting a spinnaker. They were soon, however, ahead of the sole sloop rigged Maxi, *Uruguay Natural* (formerly *Martela*) the German Frers design from the previous race which turned turtle when her keel fell off on the fourth leg.

Not surprisingly, the last to cross the starting line was *Hetman Sahaidachny*, the Ukrainian Farr designed Whitbread 60, skippered by Eugene Platon. Her skipper took her high out of the line, into the spectator craft and after a mile hoisted a huge blue and yellow masthead gennaker. As it filled, *Hetman Sahaidachny* jumped a couple of knots faster and began to overhaul *Uruguay Natural*.

It wasn't exactly the day that the sailors might have asked for. By the time of the start, the rain had long gone and the penetrating damp was beginning to diminish, but it was still grey. The Race organisers must have patted themselves on the back for making the decision, a long time previously, to start the boats to the east, to provide greater safety for the competitors and spectators alike. With the wind in the north-west, the spinnaker start was indeed a spectacle.

Tokio led *Winston* around the Heineken buoy and behind them the order was *New Zealand Endeavour, Yamaha, La Poste, Merit Cup, Dolphin & Youth, Brooksfield, Fortuna, Galicia, Intrum Justitia, US Women's Challenge, Uruguay Natural* and, bringing up the rear, *Hetman Sahaidachny*.

Suddenly, there were two men up the mast of *Winston* as things went very wrong when they peeled spinnakers. The sheet came off and as the sail flapped, the halyard jumped the masthead sheave and became jammed. Bowman Dean Phipps went up to cut it free but could not engage the gantline from the hounds to the masthead. Alexis de Cenival, the other bowman, first stood on Phipps' shoulders and then climbed the rest of the way to the masthead to cut the halyard and then began to reeve another.

Tokio's lead, therefore, increased, but *Winston* was still in second place as they passed Bembridge Ledge buoy and by then *La Poste* was ahead of *New Zealand Endeavour* and *Merit Cup* with *Fortuna* picking up speed with a gigantic mizzen gennaker set. *Galicia '93 Pescanova, Brooksfield, Yamaha* and *Dolphin & Youth* were closely bunched and then there was a gap back to the *US Women's Challenge* and the tailenders, *Uruguay Natural* and *Hetman Sahaidachny*.

The course angle to Ushant was 230° and the boats were able to hold shy spinnakers on this leg. The Maxis, however, reached high towards Ventnor pier, in order to cheat what unfavourable current was left, while the Whitbread 60s held low, aiming to be deep into the main ebb current when it began to run in the Channel. The move was a paying one as the W-60s were still ahead when they reached the French coast, with *Tokio* holding the lead.

Before the start, Dennis Conner, at a press conference, explained the reason he wanted to take part in the race. 'It's the standard of competition,' he said, 'to race in level boats around the world, has to be exciting.' As he contemplated the start, he said, 'I wouldn't mind being three feet to leeward of *Tokio* as the gun fires,' adding, 'but Dicko is not the only competitor in the Whitbread.'

It was evident at Ocean Village Marina before the start that a few of the boats were better prepared than others. With a whole day to go to the start, the four Maxi ketches together with *Tokio, Yamaha* and *Winston* were virtually deserted, their crews having completed all their tasks, while on the others there was feverish activity to have the boats ready for the morrow. That state of preparedness was reflected two days later when the position reports began to appear, courtesy of the BT Results Service.

The start was an occasion to provide irrefutable evidence that sponsorship has fully pervaded this sport in general, and this race in particular. All but three boats; *US Women's Challenge, Hetman Sahaidachny* and *New Zealand Endeavour*, are named for their main sponsors and all were 'branded' with minor sponsors' names and logos on their hulls and sails. Additionally the sponsors had taken vessels out to the course to entertain their clients and suppliers and show off their entries in this race. These vessels were also 'branded' with banners and bunting, aiming to grab a piece of the action because, due to television coverage, a yachting event had now become as big a promotional opportunity as any major sporting fixture. In global terms, the Whitbread had come of age commercially. Because of this awareness, *Dolphin & Youth* was able to secure a last minute sponsorship from Reebok, a billion dollar international company. Reebok's position in the sporting world is well known and it is a British founded company as its logo, with a Union Jack included, would adequately demonstrate. Its spokesman, Darryl Freedman said, 'We are proud to be supporting a British entry.' He also indicated that he realised the commercial value of the race.

The race was only 25 hours old when the first casualty was announced. Running in 24 knots of wind, the bumpkin on *Fortuna* gave way and the wing mizzen mast, loaded with a huge gennaker, snapped off. The crew, all unhurt in this incident, recovered the sails and ditched the glassfibre mast. At the time, *Fortuna* was south east of the Chenal du Four, the inside passage at Ushant, battling for the lead in the Maxis, with *New Zealand Endeavour* only 200 yards away.

As *Fortuna* had lost her HF and VHF aerials, it was ironically Dalton, with whom Smith had been trading insults all summer, who gave the information to Race Headquarters in Southampton. *Fortuna* continued to race, but was considerably slower without the power of the mizzen sails. Using her INMARSAT communications, Smith was able to contact Jane Powys, the shore manager, back at base and begin to organise a replacement. Designer, Javier Visiers was on the plane home to Barcelona, but was soon in discussion with Smith.

The following morning, Jane Powys said that they were 'In communication with Carbospars over a replacement.' Getting the 100 ft wing mast to Montevideo would provide a logistical problem, but one which could be overcome. Damon Roberts of Carbospars confirmed that they could build a replacement within the timescale demanded, 'It will take us four weeks to have one ready for shipping.' That shipping, organised by the official shippers Peter & May, would have almost certainly been by air. The firm which specialises in this type of movement, Heavylift of Stanstead Airport, declared there would be no difficulty in getting the spar to Montevideo. 'There is 120 ft of cargo floor on the Antonov AN-124,' said a spokesman, 'and in four weeks time, we will have plenty of aircraft available for that sort of transport.'

Describing the dismasting, Lawrie Smith recalled, 'The noise was deafening. First there was a graunching of aluminium, then a bang, followed by the tearing of glassfibre as the top 80 ft of *Fortuna*'s mast came tumbling down. The failure came not in the rig, but the tubular alloy bumpkin sticking 20 ft out behind *Fortuna*'s stern which carried the heavy sheet and backstay loads. We had sensed no problems with the design during extensive trials before the race, often in heavy weather. But just as we were enjoying our moment of glory, the whole structure folded up like a perambulator. The mizzen mast, loaded up with our giant red and white mizzen spinnaker, lurched forward and in a trice, *Fortuna*'s chances of winning lay in a cat's cradle around our ears.'

At the time, the winds were blowing 25 knots from astern and *Fortuna*, the heaviest yacht with the largest sail plan, was romping along at more than 14 knots. Others like *New Zealand Endeavour* with seemingly more fragile alloy rigs, had prudently pulled down their mizzen spinnakers and were sailing two knots slower. 'Within two hours, we would have been over their horizon,' the *Fortuna* skipper claimed. Luckily, no one was injured, but for Smith, the most sickening aspect was that their performance had blown away any doubts about the boat and memories of competing in the Fastnet Race a month before when the Spanish Maxi finished ignominiously behind all her Whitbread rivals.

Fortuna continued in the race for two days but executives from the Spanish tobacco company Tabacalara, sponsoring the yacht, vetoed the £150,000 cost and ordered the crew to turn back. With little chance of winning, they decided it was sending good money after bad. They were not to know what was to happen next. As *Fortuna* approached the spot where her mizzen had folded, there was another loud explosion, which Smith, off watch below, was sure was the boom breaking. It wasn't. The first of the sounds had been a block in the running backstay tackle giving way and that was followed by the sounds of the mast breaking. Smith could scarcely believe his bad luck. The broken spar was jettisoned to stop it puncturing the hull in the seaway that was running and *Fortuna* was motored back to Hamble, stopping first at Dartmouth to take on fuel.

The next casualty was *Brooksfield*, whose rudder stock snapped. Skipper Guido Maisto immediately headed for Brest using emergency steering – one of the safety features demanded to be proved by the race organisers – in order to meet up with her spare rudder. This was in Hamble and was despatched by the official carriers, DHL, and it was waiting for *Brooksfield* when she arrived. A fast turn around was completed and *Brooksfield* was back in the race within 18 hours of the incident.

Two days into the race, the leaders were ranged over 60 miles in an east-west line; *La Poste* was on the left wing and *Yamaha* on the right. *Merit Cup* was credited with the least distance still to go, by a mile from *Tokio* and another mile behind were *Intrum Justitia* and *Yamaha*. *Winston* was a further three miles astern, just two miles ahead of *New Zealand Endeavour*. The rest ranged back to *Hetman Sahaidachny*, 65 miles behind *Merit Cup*.

Shrouding a mystery

In the Doldrums, the heat was intense at times and a pong aboard *New Zealand Endeavour* made it all the more unbearable. The source was tracked down to the boots of crewman David Brooke, and they were unceremoniously dumped on deck to air. Two days later, the crew came to hoist the 'drifter' and were hit by the real culprit – the decomposed body of a flying fish which had become wrapped in the sail when it had been doused five days before. 'And they never even apologised,' complained Brooke of his crewmates.

By the time the leg was over, there were many interesting descriptions of it from the skippers. 'Tough,' 'Stressful,' 'Interesting,' 'Bad dose of Doldrums,' – were the remarks of Conner, Dalton, Fehlmann and Field soon after they had docked in Punta del Este. Almost every one of the 13 skippers who arrived in a four day period had slightly different tales to tell, but all were agreed that the standard of competition in this race had never been higher, nor had it been faster, as the results were to prove conclusively.

Grant Dalton's *New Zealand Endeavour* and Chris Dickson's *Tokio* took the two Heineken Trophies for this leg in their respective classes and both demolished the record time set by *Steinlager 2* in this race four years ago. *New Zealand Endeavour*, the leading Maxi, was 1 day, 13 hours 27 minutes and 25 seconds quicker than '*Big Red*'; while *Tokio*, the front-runner in the Whitbread 60 class, crossed the line 3 hours and 9 minutes later.

Within 20 hours, 7 boats were home and with the wind beginning to tail off, the gate was effectively shut for the rest and many believed that there was no way back in for the 7 who had still to finish. They pointed, historically, to the previous race, but added that with the standard of competition being considerably greater than it was in 1989, there was less need for big margins.

Dalton could, to some extent, feel cushioned from the next Maxi, Pierre Fehlmann's *Merit Cup*, which finished, in the pouring rain, 8 hours 22 minutes after *New Zealand Endeavour*. It was a similar margin that Fehlmann had finished behind Blake four years earlier, but then there was the difference between a ketch and a sloop to explain it; this time that did not exist. Fehlmann said that in strong downwind conditions, his boat was measurably slower and that in moderate reaching conditions, Dalton had consistently sailed at two tenths of a knot faster.

It was in the early evening that *New Zealand Endeavour* finished, hard on the wind, into Punta del Este. The crew were all on deck and the welcome from the Uruguayan seaside holiday resort was warm and generous. The Whitbread fleet was back in their port and Dalton was their hero. The crowds gathered on the dock as the Kiwis began their celebrations. For some of them, it was the same mixture as before – they had been on *Steinlager 2* – but the result was more poignant for Dalton, who had chased Blake all the way round the world and had entered Punta at the end of the first leg as a sloop, not a ketch as he had started.

'When we passed the latitude where we lost our mizzen in the last race,' Dalton commented,' I breathed a sigh of relief.' At that time, *New Zealand Endeavour* was some 240 miles behind where *Steinlager 2* had been. It was the last four days of the leg which were to prove the most devastating with continuously strong easterlies blowing the boats down the Brazilian coast and the total absence of the notorious calms and light weather off Rio de Janeiro allowing them to sail in three days what had taken the leaders five days in the previous race.

'The weather was not typical of the source data,' said Dalton, adding, 'the northeast Trades were very weak and the south-east Trades were more in the east than they are normally.' While the latter may have helped the boats to a fast time, the absence of 18-20 knot winds in the north-east Trades, where the conditions were 'sloppy,' most certainly put the boats well back on their calculations.

Dalton explained that his strategy for the leg had centred around the Doldrums. 'You have to get through there in the shortest possible time.' It was here that he found that it was not a leader's race. 'At times, we had leads of 70, 130 and 200 miles on *Yamaha*, but then we would run into a light patch and she would come screaming up on us and absorb almost all the lead we had established. In the end we crept away and were 150 miles clear.' It was painfully obvious that the Doldrums had been a worrying part of the race. What he had done to reduce the damage to his lead was to sail due south from the moment the unstable weather of the ITCZ was encountered. 'That way, you are through it fastest, even if you do not sail your best angles, or the best course to the finish.'

There were other hardships in the Tropics. 'The chocolate was melting in the bilge and we had to wait some time before we were in colder climes for it to harden so that we could eat it.' Dalton and his crew could joke about that in Punta, and they did with cold tinnies of Heineken in their hands, but the deprivation of one of the small creature comforts was no fun at the time. They were racing and had one eye over their shoulders at all times. 'This is the '90s and not the handicap days of the '80s,' explained Dalton, 'the public, particularly those in New Zealand, understand that the boat out in front is the winner. That was why we opted to have a Maxi, however thrilling the Whitbread 60s might be, first home is first and we feel that we can give this to our sponsors and our supporters. We know it will be tough to stay in front of the 60s, but we have every confidence that we can.'

The boats he was most concerned about, 'and not in any particular order,' were *Tokio*, *Merit Cup*, *Winston*, *Yamaha*, *Intrum Justitia* and *La Poste*. 'The 60s are equally important, and tracking their positions shows us the relative weather patterns and confirms our own decisions. We didn't want to give anything away once we were in front. I remember eight years ago when Pierre [Fehlmann] had *UBS*, he would get ahead and then sail back to the centreline of the fleet. It meant that he could not be passed. We did much the same, although we never went far from the rhumb line.'

Dalton agreed with his fellow skippers that the regular six hourly feed of position reports of the boats had added to the competitiveness of the race. That was echoed by the man who had trailed him in the Maxis for most of the race, Pierre Fehlmann. 'There is more pressure on the skippers,' he said, 'it makes it more intensive and more interesting; the race is better for it.'

Fehlmann comes from a dinghy racing background. 'I am not an offshore man,' a slightly contradictory statement from someone skippering his fifth Whitbread campaign, 'I like to race around the buoys and now I have that every six hours. There is a new race each time the positions are reported to the fleet.' Fehlmann went on to declare that ever since he raced a Swan 65 in this event, he has been surrounded by dinghy sailors and that they have always trimmed their boats as small boat sailors do, 'only,' he said with some regret, 'the rest have caught on to the idea.'

It had not been the best of legs for the Swiss skipper. At Ushant, he picked up some weed around the keel and the Z-drive and had to wait for a day for suitable conditions to dive to clear it. He then made a mistake on the third day out by failing to go far enough to the west – *New Zealand Endeavour* gained 15 miles. But it was on the eighth day that his biggest problem manifested itself. Heavy vibration set in from the keel and rudder as *Merit Cup* was running in 25 knots of breeze. Examination through the window in front of both foils revealed nothing and there was concern on board that the bulb on the bottom of the keel might be moving. It wasn't until the first calm of the Doldrums, four days later, that Pierre was able to dive to examine the problem.

He found a folded over piece of fishing net, four metres by one, tucked around the keel close to the hull – the angle of the sight glass had prevented the crew from seeing it. The 'catch up' nature of the Doldrums had, however, allowed *Merit Cup* to close up to be level with *New Zealand Endeavour* the following day. They were about eight miles apart in an east-west line with *Merit Cup* the easterly of the two. Dalton picked up a little breeze and 12 hours later was four miles ahead and the two boats were in sight of each other when a rain squall passed between the two. *New Zealand Endeavour*, on the better side of it, picked up her skirts and was off, while *Merit Cup*, first took a header, then a calm and was six hours before she was on her way again.

'At every position report, Dalton was further ahead,' said Fehlmann, 'but every time we sailed as far as he did in the previous six hours.' *Merit Cup* was slowly sailing into the same weather pattern on the far side of the Doldrums. The two boats, however, are different. *New Zealand Endeavour* is 150 mm narrower on the waterline (330 mm narrower than *Steinlager 2*) and displaces 27,700 kg compared to *Merit Cup*'s 28,285 kg. Fehlmann reduced this displacement from the 29,800 kg at which his sistership, *La Poste*, was racing. Dalton claims that he asked Farr for a lighter boat in order to surf earlier – he recognised the difference from the previous race when *Fisher & Paykel* displaced 32,500 kg to *Steinlager 2*'s 35,500 kg. It was only when surfing came out of the equation, he holds, that *Steinlager 2* had any advantage.

The sting came out of the Maxi class when first, *Fortuna* lost her mizzen, and secondly when the mizzen mast on *La Poste* twisted so that only a small amount of sail could be set on the spar. The damage to that spar became progressively worse and Daniel Mallé and his crew sailed sufficiently well to overcome that handicap to finish only one day, eleven hours behind the winner and eighth across the line. The fourth Maxi, *Uruguay Natural*, the former *Martela*, is not in the same league as the ketches and was two and a half days behind *La Poste*, but was, nevertheless, welcomed home to Punta by the President of Uruguay, Luis Alberto Lacalle.

'Dickson sailed a fine leg,' the words of praise came from Grant Dalton. 'We took some time to catch and pass him, but he was never out of our minds.' Dickson competing in his first Whitbread, has made a showing that has not surprised those who know him. His preparation has been immaculate and based on the experience he has had with the America's Cup. He spent 8,000 miles of two-boat testing, all calibrated and recorded, assessing sails and equipment as well as crew. He built boatspeed first and then, as the start came nearer, hardened his crew with some veterans of the race, like Joe English and Jacques Vincent. In that way, he added to his own enormous talent.

Andrew Cape, the *Tokio* navigator, confirmed that they had sailed the leg as a series of six hour races. 'You can only sail in the wind that you have got, and while I looked at the forecasts, I could only be sure of what might happen in 48 hours. It meant that we would concentrate on the immediate speed and look again in six hours.' Early in the campaign, *Tokio*'s crew had sought the advice of Mike Quilter, navigator of *Steinlager 2* and now of *New Zealand Endeavour*, for weather research and this put them on the right track.

'We had a good start,' said Dickson, 'but there was a gap in our sail wardrobe (the result of not being able to measure in a couple of sails which were ruled out of class) on the first night, and we fell back. We had a few breaks offshore of Portugal, but the next day the boats inshore did well.' By this time, however, *Tokio* was the front runner of the Whitbread 60 class and there was not a lot of the race when she was ever headed. 'There were opportunities for the front boats to get further in front,' said Dickson, 'but until the Equator there were no bonus miles for being in front.'

Life on board *Tokio* was definitely Spartan. 'Yes, we had books,' said the skipper, 'and the crew now know all the flag signals and a great deal about the maintenance of the water maker. The medical handbook is a favourite read.' Surplus weight had been eliminated – there was even a choice of boots or shoes, not both. Jacques Vincent had lost one shoe overboard during a sail change and had no replacement. If there was an absence of television pictures from *Tokio*, it was because Dickson decided against a SatCom A, although he had to take a lead weight to compensate for it, because, after weighing up the time needed to operate the system, he felt that it could be better used in making the boat faster.

Behind *Tokio*, there was a four-way fight for second place with each of its protagonists having a purple patch at one time or another. Sometimes they were in sight of one another, at other times the phalanx spread across 120 miles of ocean in an east-west axis. *Yamaha*, very early in the piece, had recorded what became the best 24 hour run of the leg. She was four days out when she completed 343.69 miles in a day and was presented with the Omega yellow flag at the end of the leg. Dennis Conner's *Winston* came close to this figure three days out from the finish, when down the Brazilian coast, just South of Rio de Janeiro, she clocked 343.20 miles.

Yamaha, Winston, Galicia '93 Pescanova and *Intrum Justitia* sailed all the way from the Doldrums to the finish in a series of individual surges to the front of their group. *Yamaha* had been 90 miles behind the bunch at the Equator but, by staying to the east, had made big gains to rejoin the group. *Winston* made her way to the front with her near record day but even with the close proximity of the boats as they approached the finish, there were well defined and different weather patterns. Matthew Mason, one of *Winston's* crew, provided an example.

'We were running in close company with *Yamaha* and *Galicia '93 Pescanova*, when the Spanish boat began to slide off to leeward. It was a deliberate action. When she was out of sight, *Galicia* gybed and headed inshore. We waited for the next position report (six hours later) and found to our horror that the Spaniards were 20 miles ahead of us.' He added, 'They must have had some knowledge of a stronger breeze that we didn't have.'

There are many weather stations from which navigators can draw their information and those who speak Spanish have a definite advantage down the South American coastline. It is the ones closest to the locality that provide the best information.

'The Equator to Punta was catch-up time for us,' said Ross Field, skipper of *Yamaha*, 'we were badly treated there – we got a second hiding and were 140 miles behind *Tokio*. They did all that in one day!' It meant that *Yamaha's* crew had to push the boat harder than they might otherwise have liked and there was very little sleep for a fortnight.

A day out from the finish, Field saw *Winston* charging up from astern with a masthead spinnaker set; her crew peeled to a fractional as *Yamaha* changed up the other way. The breeze was building over 30 knots and rising fast. Suddenly the topmast backstay tackle gave way and the mast lurched forward. Only smart action by Joey Allen, cutting the spinnaker halyard with his knife, saved the spar. But it also saved *Yamaha* from the type of broach that *Winston* suffered as she was caught lowering her fractional kite with the wind in excess of 50 knots. 'At that time,' said Field, 'we were running with just the mainsail at over 20 knots.'

Meantime, *Galicia* had slipped away to finish 10 hours behind *Tokio* and an hour ahead of *Yamaha*. *Winston* crossed the line two and a quarter hours later, with *Intrum Justitia* another three hours behind. A whole day passed before Matt Humphries brought *Dolphin & Youth* to the finish.

'We took the inside passage at Ushant and were second at that stage, but when we went to the east, it proved to be a mistake.' That mistake was compounded in the light to moderate winds where *Dolphin & Youth*, with a shortage in her sail wardrobe, was not as fast as the leaders and her problems were soon to be magnified. 'At the Doldrums, we were 40 miles behind *Yamaha* but it was then that we lost the use of our Weatherfax,' said Humphries. Without the weather information (Humphries said that the routing weather supplied by the race office was simply not enough) *Dolphin & Youth* began to slip back.

Brooksfield was to catch up some of the deficit she incurred when putting into Brest for a replacement rudder, and for the last eleven days of the race was 'more or less' in sight of *Dolphin & Youth*. It was only by using their track, on the six hourly positions that gave Humphries and his navigator, Steve Hales, any guide to the weather. *Dolphin & Youth* held off the Italians' challenge and led them across the finishing line by 13 minutes. Humphries stepped ashore with a black eye. 'I was decked by a runner block when I went to look to leeward,' he explained and admitted that he had been knocked out by the blow.

Dolphin & Youth and *Brooksfield* had had more than their fair share of light winds in their last day; fickle breezes that did not affect the first seven boats to finish, but the *US Women's Challenge* had even more and it was 40 hours after *Brooksfield* that the red hulled Whitbread 60 crossed the line just before dawn, three and a half days behind *Tokio*. It was not, however, a bad result for the all-women crew. 'The main tore nine times,' said skipper, Nance Frank, 'we had about 68 hours of down time.'

Leah Newbold, the New Zealand sailmaker on board, said, 'the main was up and down like a yo-yo and we were doing repair work while it was still up as well.' The *US Women's Challenge* has been badly hit by a limited budget, but that mainsail was not needed for the second leg. Frank negotiated with David Glen, the shore manager of *Yamaha*, from whom she chartered the boat in the first place, for the purchase of one of *Yamaha*'s spare mainsails.

When *Hetman Sahaidachny* arrived twelve hours after the *US Women's Challenge*, skipper Eugene Platon announced that the yacht would be retiring from the race due to lack of funds. It had suffered keel problems on the first leg with a composite part of the bulb slowly breaking away. This had first slowed the boat and then the upcoming repairs had been contributory to the decision to withdraw as there were no funds to pay for this. Then, less than 24 hours later, Platon announced that *Hetman Sahaidachny* was back in the race following a $120,000 sponsorship from Victor Zjerditski of Gradobank. This enabled the Ukranians to compete in the second leg. Only their countrymen in *Odessa-Moscow Times* still remained at sea and were not expected to finish until a week before the restart.

Staple diet

When Anatoly Verba, skipper of *Odessa* finally arrived, he admitted that he had had trouble selling eastern bloc fare to his Western crewmates during the first leg. After running out of freeze dried food as well as cooking gas a week out from Punta del Este, the crew were forced to live on a diet of potatoes and baked beans. British crewman Tony Pink, who joined the yacht at the last minute, lost considerable weight during the 6,000 miles voyage. 'I was very seasick for the first week when we were fighting our way through a big storm in the Bay of Biscay, and for the last week, I have only had one meal a day,' he complained.

Not surprisingly perhaps, he decided in Uruguay not to continue the voyage while another Ukrainian crew member jumped ship to join Eugene Platon's rival entry *Hetman Sahaidachny*.

PR executives from Heineken and Champagne Mumm were at loggerheads in Punta del Este over what should be sprayed over arriving crews. The Dutch brewers who spent upwards of $5 million on the race promoting the brand that gets to parts that other beers can't reach, were understandably miffed when cameras and crews continually focused on the local Champagne Mumm girls. To the delight of arriving crews, their white trousers turned see-through when touched by champagne and the girls were eventually banned from the arrival pontoon.

Undaunted, they greeted the crews from an inflatable for the next arrival and were eagerly pulled aboard. 'Spraying beer over is a bit tacky,' complained one crewman.

'I only drink champagne – and in a glass please,' said Nance Frank when her girls crew arrived in port. That was enough to turn Heineken executives as green as their beer cans.

Mutiny, malcontent and misfortune

It was little anticipated that the first Uruguayan stop-over would become a turmoil of bitterness, anger, frustration and disappointment instead of a relaxing interlude.

Sebastian Rana, a young Uruguayan had been hugged as a hero by his President when his yacht *Uruguay Natural* arrived from Southampton a month earlier. However, he began to have doubts about this dip down into the Southern Ocean as the yacht left the dock but others among his crew restrained him from getting back ashore. He finally 'snapped' shortly before the ten minute gun and jumped overboard into the arms of his girl-friend who had also jumped from a shadowing spectator boat

More intriguing was the forced replacement of Nance Frank, skipper of the *US Women's Challenge* by fellow American Dawn Riley, a former crew from Tracy Edwards' 1989/90 Whitbread Round the World Race entry *Maiden*. The rumblings of discontent, which began in Southampton when Frank's *Challenge* came close to being chained to the dock by a group of disgruntled creditors, came to a head soon after they docked at Punta del Este. Finnish watch leader Mikaela von Koskull and Australian navigator Adrienne Cahalan decided to leave the yacht, and when British physiotherapist Sue Crafer followed them a day later, Frank was forced to withdraw her entry from the race.

At one point, it was thought that the girls might have sunk their differences by promoting Mikaela von Koskull and French yachtswomen Michel Paret as joint sailing skippers, but while this was acceptable to most of the crew, Frank refused to accept any demotion of her role.

The move to oust Frank was orchestrated by Ocean Ventures Management, the owners of the boat and also responsible for Ross Field's third placed New Zealand entry *Yamaha*. The company formerly repossessed the boat without Frank's knowledge, then put forward a proposal to the Whitbread race organisers that would enable the yacht to continue under a new skipper with four new crew members.

The race rules allowed for only 20 percent of the crew to be changed per leg. Ian Bailey-Willmot the race director exercised his discretion, allowed within the rules, to a larger number of crew changes because experience onboard would not be diminished. 'I believe that it is in the best interests of the race, the majority of the crew and women's sailing to allow the boat to continue.' he conceded.

Riley, a member of Bill Koch's America's Cup squad, headed for New York airport the moment clearance was given and was joined onboard by fellow *Maiden* veterans Jeni Mundy from Britain and French yachtswoman Marie-Claude Kieffer. Lisa Beecham, an Australian doctor who sailed aboard the boat in the Fastnet Race back in August and had been acting as shore manager to the crew, was the fourth new recruit.

They replaced Susan Chiu, who had underwritten Frank's challenge to date, together with fellow Americans Barbara Span and Vanessa Linsley. Michele Paret, another *Maiden* veteran, decided to leave the crew for personal reasons. 'It has been a very difficult time, but this decision is something I have to live with for the rest of my life', she said.

Tracy Edwards, who skippered *Maiden*, the first all-women crew in the previous race four years before, welcomed the changes. Pulling no punches, she said, 'Nance Frank was such a waste of space. If women's sailing is going to be promoted, it has to be done properly and Dawn Riley is the one to do it. I was so frightened that after all we did to raise the profile of women within the sport that Frank was going to drag it back into the gutter. The choice of Dawn is the best thing to have happened to the project. It will be in good hands from now on.'

Explaining the role of the yacht's owners, spokesman David Glen said, 'It became obvious Nance Frank was never going to be able to pay the charter fee, so we have helped to restructure the crew in anticipation of getting sponsorship by the time they reach Fremantle in December.'

Frank returned to America threatening to have the yacht impounded, telling supporters that charter payments were up to date and the next instalment had not been due until 7 January. 'They have taken my boat, they have taken my belongings. They have even taken my tooth brush,' she complained. 'Our boat has been stolen from us and we want it back.'

David Glen agreed that the payment was not an issue. 'The decision to repossess the boat was not taken lightly and not until after Nance Frank had withdrawn her entry from the race. We have taken legal advice and only did it once it was realised that she would never be in a position to pay us the remaining fees.' Asked about Frank's legal threats, he said, 'We can't dismiss that risk, but we don't believe it will happen.' He could not have been more wrong.

Another question mark hovered over the continuation of Anatoly Verba's penniless Ukrainian entry *Odessa*, which had set out from Southampton five days behind the fleet and lost a further 12 days en route. Tony Pink decided to drop out and another Ukrainian crewmember jumped ship to join Eugene Platon's rival entry *Hetman Sahaidachny*. 'In America, they say I am a millionaire, owning a boat worth $1.3 million, but here in Uruguay, I don't even have enough money to buy food,' said Verba forlornly as he tried to recruit new crew members. He eventually sailed with just eight crew onboard, failing to wait for a new boom flown out to replace their broken spar, and a split in the topmast.

Other crews also faced problems getting equipment and sails, held up in Customs at Montevideo. Daniel Mallé's crew from the French maxi *La Poste* came close to leaving without their freeze-dried food supplies and a large number of new sails built for the Southern Ocean had measurers up burning the midnight oil on the eve of the start.

Another late arrival was British yachtsman Lawrie Smith who flew out to Uruguay one week before re-start to take over as skipper of the European entry *Intrum Justitia*. The Olympic bronze medalist, who skippered the fourth placed Maxi *Rothmans* in this race four years ago, took over from the Swedish Whitbread veteran Roger Nilson after he had been hospitalised with an infected knee.Smith, who began the race as skipper of the ill-fated Spanish Maxi *Fortuna* forced to retire from the race within a week of the start, joined fellow *Fortuna* crewman Paul Standbridge who had signed on with the *Intrum* crew the previous week.

The 37-year-old skipper said, 'I'm thrilled to be back in the race and can't wait for the Southern Ocean, but it is a great shame that this has happened to Roger Nilson.' His knee had began to swell up during the last few days of the first leg and when his condition got worse during the stop-over, Nilson was

ABOVE *Tokio* leads away from the start at Southampton on a grey September Saturday. *Mark Pepper/PPL.* BELOW Eric Tabarly steers while Daniel Malle looks on as *La Poste*, with a depleted crew, sails away from Fort Lauderdale. *Mark Pepper/PPL*

ABOVE The *Tokio* crew look on smiling as skipper Chris Dickson sprays the celebratory Mumm after winning leg 1. *Mark Pepper/PPL.* BELOW Regular soaking when sailing a W-60 downwind, on board *Intrum Justitia* in the Southern Ocean. *Rick Tomlinson/PPL*

Heineken and the all-women crew arriving at Punta del Este at the end of leg 4.
Mark Pepper/PPL

The happiness that goes with winning; navigator Marcel van Triest and skipper Lawrie Smith at the end of the second leg in Fremantle. *Barry Pickthall/PPL*

The raw end of *New Zealand Endeavour's* broken mizzen mast at the end of leg 2.
Mark Pepper/PPL

New Zealand Endeavour, just short of Auckland, on her way to winning the third leg.
Mark Pepper/PPL

flown back to Stockholm where he underwent surgery and intensive treatment for the infection. The Swede, a doctor by profession, decided that it would be unwise for him to continue in the race. 'I'm very sad that I will be unable to continue, but wish the crew and Lawrie the best of luck' he said from his hospital bed. *Intrum Justitia* finished a disappointing fifth on the first stage from Southampton to Punta del Este, and Smith and Standbridge were seen as key elements in closing the 15 hour gap on Chris Dickson's first placed 60 footer *Tokio*.

6

LEG TWO *Punta del Este to Fremantle*
Drama, duelling and dissent

From the start Lawrie Smith stamped his authority the second leg of the race and demonstrated his wealth of experience in high level yacht racing by calling the shots while Pierre Mas steered to be first across the line and first around the turning mark three miles down the track at Punta Ballena.

The switch of skippers was very much a last minute affair; as Smith commented on arrival a day before the restart. 'A week is a long time in yacht racing. Last Friday, I was at home in Lymington, planning a family holiday in Scotland. Now, I am in Punta del Este in a race against time getting to know a new boat and crew before the start today of the second, harshest stage of the Whitbread Round the World Race.'

The call to skipper the European Whitbread 60 entry came one week earlier. Richard Butcher, a lawyer friend and former Fireball world champion, burnt the midnight oil drawing up a contract and Smith was on the first available flight out to Uruguay, arriving there with five days to spare. The change of skipper was as much a surprise to the crew as it was to Smith himself.

The brilliant yellow spinnaker of *Intrum Justitia* was the one bright feature of an otherwise grey day. Rain fell quite heavily as the 14 competing yachts, began to leave the breakwater of Punta harbour. There were the usual fond farewells but these were muted by the inclemency of the weather and there was a notable hastening by those who were not going on the race to return to reasonable shelter. For those who were going, it was a soggy beginning to what was bound to be a wet and cold leg.

At 7,558 nautical miles, it was the longest leg of the Whitbread, one which took the fleet deep in to the Roaring Forties and Furious Fifties, the Great Circle course optimally taking them to 52.4° south on the first half of the leg. This time, the leg to Fremantle had the addition of Prince Edward Islands as a turning mark, at 46° south, just over half way across the Southern Ocean. The second Great Circle course drops to just 50° south; the aim of this exercise is to keep the yachts clear of the pack ice, this year its limit was at 56° south.

The importance of the Whitbread to Uruguay was exemplified when the country's President, Luis Alberto Lacalle, was at the start to fire the gun which sent the competitors on their way. He had earlier been in Punta to greet the crew of *Uruguay Natural* when they arrived at the end of the first leg and this time he saw them make a creditable start in this highly competitive field.

Intrum Justitia started at the committee boat end of the line, and first to have a spinnaker up and drawing, was soon out ahead of the fleet. There may well have been a smile on Smith's face at this point, but with a forecast of the 20 knot south-easter increasing as a result of a Pampero to 60 knots at nightfall, there may have been a certain apprehension within him and the rest of the competitors.

The conditions were just right for the ketches and it was not long before Grant Dalton with *New Zealand Endeavour* and Daniel Mallé aboard *La Poste* were chasing the leader hard. Within seconds of the start the spinnaker on *Winston*, Dennis Conner's Whitbread 60 (skippered for this leg by Brad Butterworth) had blown out and a new one set to replace it. It lost *Winston* some time and Chris Dickson in *Tokio* was quick to take advantage and move into fourth place on the water.

It was three miles to the Punta Ballena turning mark and not more than a quarter of an hour had elapsed before Smith called for the spinnaker to be doused and turned hard on the wind with the windward water ballast tanks of *Intrum Justitia* fully loaded. He made the turn just inside *New Zealand Endeavour*, with *La Poste* trailing a boat-length behind. Then came *Tokio*, *Winston* and the Italian entry, *Brooksfield*. Ross Field in *Yamaha* just edged out Pierre Fehlmann's *Merit Cup* with Javier de la Gandara in *Galicia '93 Pescanova* next.

Eugune Platon misjudged the turn with *Hetman Sahaidachny*, hitting the buoy and cutting it free. British skipper Matt Humphries in *Dolphin & Youth* managed to slip round outside both the boat and the buoy but the next three, *Odessa-Moscow Times*, *Uruguay Natural* and *Women's Challenge* (now no longer prefaced by US) had to chase the drifting mark before rounding it.

Just before the start, one of the crew of *Uruguay Natural*, Sebastian Rana, deliberately jumped overboard. He was picked up by a spectator boat, leaving the Maxi-sloop one short for the Southern Ocean leg.

The strong winds forecasted for the first night did not materialise and the fleet adopted a port tack, heading south. A split developed when nine of the boats tacked to starboard during that first night and, for a time, the most easterly boat, *Hetman Sahaidachny*, was credited as fleet leader by the race results computer. Chris Dickson in *Tokio* led *Brooksfield* and the *Women's Challenge* with their new skipper, Dawn Riley, in the group of five that went to the south. The rest tacked back on to a southerly course, after a wind shift, and were some 50 miles east-north-east of *Tokio* after two days at sea.

By then all were enjoying a north-easterly air stream of 10 – 12 knots and the forecast was for an increase the further south they went, and to back to the north-west. It would depend on just when and how the change took place as to whether Dickson's strategy was successful. Closely grouped together on the right flank were *Merit Cup* and *New Zealand Endeavour*, hotly pursued by *Intrum Justitia*, *Galicia '93 Pescanova* and *Winston*. Taking a less extreme course were *Yamaha* and *La Poste*, almost midway between the two groups.

The second leg had been artificially split into two distinct sections by the inclusion of the Prince Edward Islands at 46° south, as a mark of the course, to be passed to starboard. The Islands are approximately 4,000 miles from the start and 3,500 from the finish at Fremantle. It was the last 1,000 miles into Fremantle which proved to be crucial, as they were four years earlier when *Fisher & Paykel*, which had led for most of the way from Punta, was passed by three boats, losing more than 200 miles in the process.

Before the start of this leg, Brad Butterworth, who had been a watchleader on *Steinlager 2*, when she won the leg in 1989, said that he expected a close finish. 'It would not surprise me,' he said, 'if the leading Whitbread 60s were not in a close line abreast with a 1,000 miles to go. The one who gets the break then will win easily.' It took *Steinlager 2* 27 days 5 1/2 hours to complete the second leg last time, but many of the skippers were predicting 25 1/2 days would be all that they would need this time – how right they were to be. More speculation settled around whether it would be a Whitbread 60 or a Maxi that would win the leg. The general opinion was that this would be one opportunity for the Whitbread 60s to excel – again, how right this would prove to be.

Just three days into the second leg, the cry of 'Man Overboard' went up from Chris Dickson's Whitbread 60, *Tokio* at midday local time (1500 GMT) when the wind was 15-20 knots. The chilling cry was for Japanese bowman Ken Hara who had gone over the side during a spinnaker change and the incident underlined the need for constant vigilance and regular safety orders on board the boats, particularly in the Southern Ocean.

Bowman Hara had climbed out to the end of the spinnaker pole to spike off the old spinnaker as the new sail filled. It was a regular manoeuvre, one which he had performed several times every day during this race. Unfortunately, as he climbed back along the pole, he slipped. Aboard *Tokio* there is a standing rule that every member of the crew who is working outboard of the life-lines, should be clipped on with their harnesses. Hara was not attached and, as a result, he fell into the water.

Safety Fast - Staying alive in the Southern Ocean.

Within a week of the Whitbread fleet leaving Punta del Este on the second stage of this round the world race to Fremantle, Australia, two Man Overboard incidents brought home the very real dangers of racing in the icy waters of the Southern Ocean.

The lesson for 30-year-old Ken Hara, the Japanese bowman aboard Chris Dickson's Whitbread 60 *Tokio* was to clip on. For fellow bowman Craig Watson aboard *New Zealand Endeavour*, it was to take a deep breath. Both went for a ducking while riding the end of a spinnaker pole during sail changes. Watson, who had taken the precaution of clipping on his harness, was dragged through the freezing waters at 15 knots for more than a minute after the spinnaker he was about to release suddenly exploded, and the pole dropped down. Mercifully, the New Zealander was eventually plucked from the water by his crewmates cold, but uninjured. Hara, too, has been counting his lucky stars that it was daylight when he went overboard and that the crew had practised their recovery manoeuvre several times before.

Chris Dickson reported: 'As bowman, Ken had to climb out two metres to the end of the spinnaker pole with the new spinnaker, clip on to the end of the pole, wait for it to be hoisted and then spike off the old sail. This is a common manoeuvre that happens up to ten times a day and Ken was at the end of the pole for about one minute. Having spiked off the old spinnaker, he was climbing down the rope from the pole back to the boat when he fell and was not able to hold on.

Ian Stewart called out "Ken! where is he?" which was when we saw him floating away from the boat. We were doing 13 knots away from him with two spinnakers hoisted and a lot of work to do before we could turn the boat round. The call was made below decks - "Man Overboard. All hands on deck!" The Man Overboard button was pushed on our GPS satellite navigation system to give us an exact position, range and bearing back to Hara. The life ring with light and drogue was thrown but he was already too far away to reach it. A hand-held EPIRB (Emergency Position Indicating Radio Beacon) was activated and thrown astern to give another locating method. Kelvin Harrop took up station at the stern to keep visual watch and all the crew resumed normal positions with me at the helm calling commands to best manoeuvre the boat.

With all crew on deck, the first, then second spinnaker was lowered and the boat tacked within a minute. We then sailed back down the reverse course with navigator Andrew Cape calling the bearing. Hara was sighted exactly where we had expected and the boat stopped alongside. Ropes were ready on both sides and he was pulled back on board unhurt within five minutes of going overboard.'

Dickson emphasised that the incident occurred because of carelessness, not extreme conditions. 'It is standard practice on *Tokio* for the bowman to clip on when working outside the lifelines. Hara was wearing his bowman's climbing harness, but was not clipped on.'

It was a timely lesson for all crews. 'It certainly made my guys think more about safety,' said Smith, now the skipper of *Intrum Justitia*.

The Whitbread race is perhaps unique in that if a man is lost overboard, the yacht is deemed to have retired from the leg. 'We came under considerable pressure from skippers and crews to remove the rule,' Ian Bailey-Willmot, the race director admitted, adding, 'But it is not there because we are worried crews might not make every effort to search for their mates, it is there to reinforce the skipper's demand that his crew clip on at all times. Of the four lives lost during past races, each one has been because the men lost contact with their yacht,' he stressed.

Along with these tough rules, the Royal Naval Sailing Association under whose burgee all Whitbread races have been run, also insisted on each crewman carrying the very latest in safety equipment. First and foremost is a portable EPIRB, carried in an oil-skin pocket which sets off automatically should the man fall overboard. No larger than a cigarette packet, these compact homing beacons, transmit automatically on the 121.5 MHz emergency frequency. Once fully immersed in water they have a range of between 1-3 miles at sea level and 70-100 miles from the air. Each yacht is also equipped with a portable direction finder to lead the crew back to their man. The system, which was developed four years ago by a safety committee sponsored by *The Times* London, Whitbread, BOC and the British Steel Challenge race organisers, saved two lives during the 1989/90 race and is now produced commercially.

That same committee also highlighted the life preserving attributes of dry-suits. Tests carried out by Dr Richard Allen, head of research at the military test centre based at Farnborough, showed that they extended life expectancy in freezing waters from minutes to more than a hour. Two companies, Musto and Henri-Lloyd then met the challenge set by the Whitbread race organisers to design dry-suits suitable for ocean racing which were worn by the crews in the Southern Ocean and North Atlantic.

With their rubber cuffs and neck band to keep the water out, these suits not only keep crews dry, but the insulation they provide wards off hypothermia for an hour or more. Indeed, the Henri-Lloyd suit has a second layer which can be inflated should the wearer fall in the water, to provide both buoyancy and a second thermal barrier that extends life expectancy to more than three hours. 'These Whitbread 60s are notoriously wet. The spray flying across the deck has the power of a fire hydrant, so quite apart from any life-saving attributes, these suits were the only way to stay dry' said *Intrum*'s grateful skipper Lawrie Smith.

The excitement of setting a 375.2 mile record run on the first Thursday of the leg, was marred for *Intrum*'s crew by the injury to Magnus Olsson. He was swept off his feet by the green water constantly flooding down the deck and thrown into the cockpit, badly spraining his wrist. It proved quite a blow, for being one man down while surfing through the Roaring Forties, made it all the more taxing for the rest of the crew. Though averaging 15.6 knots between 0800 on November 17 and 18, surprisingly, the conditions were not that strong. The maximum wind strength experienced was 35 knots and that lasted for only four hours. For the rest of the time, it never blew more than 20 knots. The secret of *Intrum Justitia*'s success was the wind angle which remained constant from the south west to give her perfect broad-reaching conditions. Unlike the much heavier Maxis, the 60 footers like *Intrum Justitia* can be kept surfing at 20 knots for 15-20 minutes at a time. As a result, she pulled out a 20 mile lead over Pierre Fehlmann's *Merit Cup* and were taking 1-2 miles out of Grant Dalton's *New Zealand Endeavour* each day.

Smith commented at the time, 'Our biggest problem is the amount of water and spray washing across the deck. These boats are notoriously wet – more akin to a submarine on the point of dive, than even a surfing sailboard. It is just as wet below decks too. What water does not come in through the hatch, leaks in through the many fittings bolted on deck. *Intrum* is like a colander, and worse, the drying locker has never worked, so we are not only working, but eating and sleeping in damp clothing.'

Magnus, forever the happiest man in the world, was now below decks without his normal smile, sitting with a make-shift plaster cast supporting his arm. His injury however, reinforced in the minds of all on board the necessity of having safety harnesses clipped on at all times. When boats are running at 20 knots, the waves of water coming down the deck are like moving concrete walls that sweep everything before them. If crewmen are not clipped on there is a good chance of being knocked down – or, worse still, overboard.

Brooksfield had a brief claim to fame on November 27th, when she claimed a 24 hour run of 380 miles, but six hours later, *Yamaha* did 387.4. *Brooksfield*, however, bettered that, with 394.4 miles. At this time, the leaders were rounding Prince Edward Islands; *New Zealand Endeavour* was 65 miles ahead of *Intrum Justitia* with *Tokio* just 15 minutes behind her. It was then that van Trieste called for the move to the south that proved to be the winning strategy

Four days later, Smith reported again, 'We're on a roll! For the past six hours we have been averaging almost 20 knots in a blind but spectacular run through the Southern Ocean and are on course to set a new 24 hour record run – if these winds hold.' They did and the world monohull record went to 425 miles with Smith having a stranglehold on the Omega Trophy for this race at an average of 17.7 knots. He said that it was not what he considered to be the ultimate – 460-470 miles was possible – adding, 'and if anyone is going to do it, I suppose it will be us!' In the same period, *Tokio* sailed 415.8 miles and *Galicia '93 Pescanova* 411.7, with Javier de la Gandara beating his previous best of 403 in the last race with *Fortuna*.

With 3,000 miles to go, the rivalry between the Maxis and the W-60s was hotting up. The Maxis couldn't match the headlong dashes of the W-60s, but when the wind lightened, they were back in the hunt with longer day's runs which kept them at the forefront of the fleet. That was to end, and when it did, van Triest sent a fax to Grant Dalton claiming the wager he had with him that a Whitbread 60 would take 50 miles out of the leading Maxi in 24 hours. The reply came from 'Low Life', aka Mike Quilter, who reported that *New Zealand Endeavour* had lost the top of her mizzen - the third of the ketches to lose the aft mast.

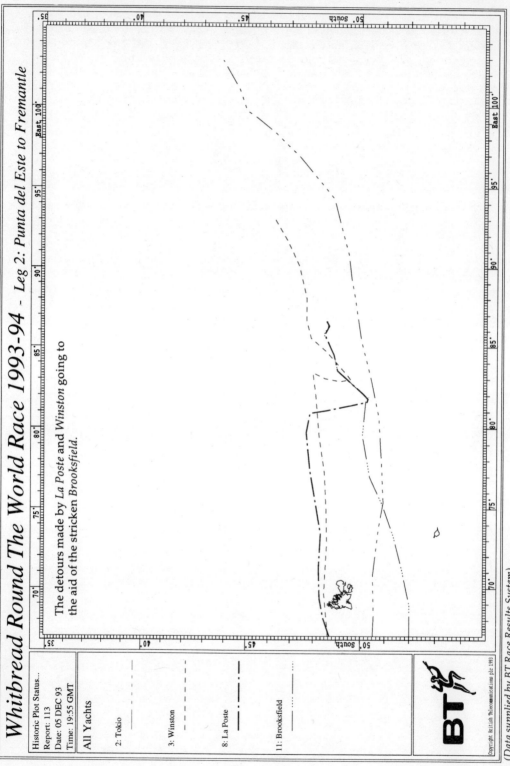

Whitbread Round The World Race 1993-94 - *Leg 2: Punta del Este to Fremantle*

Historic Plot Status...
Report: 113
Date: 05 DEC 93
Time: 19:55 GMT

The detours made by *La Poste* and *Winston* going to the aid of the stricken *Brooksfield*.

All Yachts

2: Tokio

3: Winston

8: La Poste

11: Brooksfield

Copyright British Telecommunications plc 1993

(Data supplied by BT Race Results System)

The Brooksfield rescue

A phone call received at Race Headquarters at 0815 on 3 December from the Maritime Rescue Co-ordination Centre in Canberra was the first alert that things might not be right on *Brooksfield*.

Canberra, like the Coastguard Centre at Falmouth, is one of a network of listening posts around the world that pick up the emergency signals broadcast via the Emergency Position Indicating Radio Beacon (EPIRB) carried by all shipping – and the Whitbread yachts.

As a safety device, the EPIRB is most effective. Their one problem is that in the case of yachts, the rescue authorities have no way of knowing whether the device has been knocked overboard or activated accidentally by waves sweeping across the deck. It is also not possible to determine the nature of the emergency onboard so all Ian Bailey-Willmot and his team had to go on was the position given by *Brooksfield*'s EPIRB, deep in the Southern Ocean, 2,000 miles west of Fremantle.

Earlier, the BT satellite system tracking the fleet had placed the green 60 footer in sixth place, speeding at more than 16 knots before a westerly gale. The first task was to try and raise her by radio or her INMARSAT C satellite telex link. If all had been well, the telex service should have flicked up on *Brooksfield*'s screen within seconds of it being sent from Race Headquarters but when there was no reply to this, or when the positions of all the yachts were polled, concern grew.

Other crews within the fleet were all quickly informed and two of the nearest yachts, Brad Butterworth's *Winston*, and *La Poste* skippered by Frenchman Daniel Mallé, were called on to turn back towards *Brooksfield*'s last known position 427 miles west of the Kerguelen Islands. They did so immediately.

Facing winds of 50 knots and big head seas, *La Poste*, the closest yacht, reached the area at 2245 after first spotting a blip on their radar screen. 'It was just a target. We did not know if it was them or ice, but then we saw their mast, made contact on the VHF and were relieved to hear that all were well.'

From the tearful reunion with crew members from the French yacht when both met again on the dockside at Fremantle, it was obvious that the Italians had felt lucky to be alive.

Problems began when *Brooksfield*'s rudder shaft suddenly broke after a freak wave hit the yacht. Recalling the incident later, skipper Guido Maisto said, 'It was possible that the stern could have broken up at any time. I had the safety of my crew to consider. It was very important to have some assistance as soon as possible.'

More than three tons of water flooded into the boat before they could cut away the broken rudder and seal the 35 cm wide hole with a sail bag and bucket. 'There was no panic, but it was not a very good feeling. We closed the watertight door, so knew the boat would stay afloat,' said Maisto, adding: 'We used the bilge pumps and buckets but could not reduce the level of water in the boat for three to four hours until we had fixed the hole.'

Andrea Proto, a *Brooksfield* watchleader said, 'People were up to their chests in water which was very, very cold. We also had a lot of debris floating about like fenders, ropes and sailbags, which we had to clear out to stop them hitting everyone.'

Unable to cut the steering quadrant and release the broken shaft, the crew hoisted a storm jib and gybed the boat two or three times before pressure from the water finally led to the rudder breaking off. The hole was plugged with a sail bag, a bucket wrapped in foam taken from a bunk and jammed in place with the aid of floor boards and the jockey pole which they poked up through the hole in the deck where the rudder post had been.

Of *La Poste*'s efforts to stand by them during the 70 knot storm that followed, Maisto said, 'It was good to have them nearby because we were feeling very vulnerable and not absolutely sure that the repair was strong enough. We still could have had to leave the boat.'

Once the drama was over, suggestions were raised in the Italian media that the *Brooksfield* saga had somehow been more a publicity stunt than a matter of life and death.The attack, published in the *La Republica* daily paper, and deeply resented by families and friends, suggested that both the race organisers, and *Brooksfield*'s sponsors had deliberately withheld information in the hope of milking all they could from the publicity. The inference was that if the Italian media had known that three further signals had been received from the yacht's EPIRB, (not one as suggested in the press release issued by race headquarters) the story would have been down-graded from front page headlines.

With the benefit of 20/20 hindsight, perhaps there was a case for issuing further releases as the situation developed, for the four EPIRB blips showed an hourly drift of 2.6 knots offering greater hope that Maisto and his crew were alive. Instead, the release simply informed the press and families involved that '*Brooksfield* failed to respond to the 0755 position report poll or any subsequent attempts to contact her,' leaving the impression that just one signal had been picked up from the yacht before the worst had occurred.

Meridian, the local TV station at Southampton and host broadcaster to the race, was first to break the news that further signals had been picked up from the yacht on its late night news at 2230.

This was corrected later by Ian Bailey-Willmot who confirmed that the last signal had been broadcast at 1108. He was adamant that the press statement was in essence correct. 'The last blip came in moments after we issued the release when it was too late to change it,' he said, adding, 'We had no way of knowing from those signals whether the yacht was upside down, the EPIRB buoy was floating alone in the water or the crew had it with them in a liferaft. This was a full scale emergency and I was not about to be distracted by issuing press releases until we had something more concrete to add.'

On arrival, Joao Cabeçades, *La Poste*'s Portuguese watchleader leapt to the defence of *Brooksfield*'s crew, adamant that criticism of Maisto's emergency call in the Italian media had been badly misplaced, he said. 'No one has the right to judge whether others should switch on or off their distress signal. The *Brooksfield* crew are good seamen — I have sailed with some of them before. If these guys decided to switch on a distress signal, it was the right thing to do. If it puts lives at risk or not, that is what we are here for. In a race like this, we know that we can count only on other competitors to help each other.'

After what was undoubtedly a gruelling leg there was adequate consolation for one man. Lawrie Smith sailed into Fremantle Harbour with a distinct smile on his face. The British skipper whose challenge in the Whitbread Round the World Race had fallen on its face in the first week of the race when the masts of his Maxi, *Fortuna*, had tumbled to the deck, was triumphant aboard his new charge. *Intrum Justitia* was first across the line in a time which shattered the record for the leg from Punta del Este, and, just as importantly, Smith had cut into Dickson's overall lead.

Intrum Justitia had taken 25 days 14 hours 39 minutes and 6 seconds at an average speed of 12.4 knots and was 39 hours faster that Peter Blake's time with *Steinlager 2* in the last race. In addition, the European entry had sailed 240 miles further, because of the introduction of Prince Edward Island as a mark of the course in this race. All of the first seven finishers broke the previous record time for the leg.

Almost certainly, at the back of Smith's mind, was the fact that he had achieved an overall victory in a Whitbread 60 class yacht. He had always realised the potential of these new, smaller boats and had found that if he were prepared to push one to its limits that it would beat the bigger Maxis. No one was prepared to drive a boat harder, and Smith reaped the benefit of his skill in this direction.

It was a leg on which the Whitbread 60s, even deprived of their masthead spinnakers, were able to dominate. Their ability to sail at sustained higher speeds than the Maxis when the wind was at its freshest proved to be their strength. That there was a considerable proportion of the leg spent reaching, when the W-60s were able to use their water ballast to the full, was also a contributory factor to them being able to beat the much bigger boats.

Smith was quick to acknowledge his navigator, Marcel van Triest, for his part in the victory on the 7,558 nautical mile leg. 'He made the critical interpretations of the weather,' Smith declared, 'and that was what ultimately made us the gains.' Smith cited the decision to go south immediately after passing Prince Edward Island as one of the key factors in *Intrum Justitia's* success.

Chris Dickson's *Tokio*, which eventually finished two hours behind into Fremantle, had closed an earlier gap of more than a hundred miles to just two and a half miles as they rounded the rocky outcrop at the halfway stage of the race, and was left almost 50 miles astern in a day, when van Triest convinced his skipper that they should head south for a better weather pattern.

'Marcel was certain that we should go that way, but it seemed to me that we were on the wrong tack,' said Smith, when explaining what proved to be the race winning strategy. 'He was right however,' and was definitely proved so a day later, when *Intrum Justitia* surged into a comfortable lead that was to be the basis of her ultimate victory. Van Trieste's side of it was that Smith 'moaned all night that we were on the wrong gybe and only cheered up when the next position report came through.' By then, *Intrum Justitia* was back in a comfortable lead.

Ross Field, whose *Yamaha* was third to finish, six hours after *Intrum Justitia*, had earlier declared that, at times, the race had been, 'Bordering on madness.' He was confirmed in his opinion by Smith. The British skipper's description of sailing through 'growlers,' the small bits broken off icebergs, showed how hair-raising it had been. 'We were sailing in 40 knots of wind with the spinnaker up,' he said, 'at a regular 17 knots, with growlers on either side, and we could see the lumps of ice no more than 50 feet away. And that was in the daylight,' he added, 'we could see nothing at night.' Yet Smith knew that he had to press his boat hard, as did his much trusted lieutenant, Paul Standbridge.

'They are tough little boats,' said Standbridge, who began the race with Smith aboard *Fortuna*, 'but as they are all the same, you have to sail them well.' The veteran of three previous Whitbreads said that it had been harder than anything else he had endured. 'Not physically, but mentally,' he said, explaining that it was living on an edge all the time that made it so difficult. And there were many who agreed with him.

It was easy to see a different attitude from normal at the end of this leg. The crews all arrived completely drained of energy, having given everything to utilising the fierce elemental forces to cross the Southern Ocean in the shortest possible time. Most spent little time greeting friends and loved ones, quickly packed up their boats and left to seek the solace of dry warmth and safety in their hotel rooms. Not for them an immediate foray to the pub to swap war stories and swing the lamp until they had changed the shape of the world; not this time, at least.

There had obviously been some psychological scoring made in the race. Smith said that after a week, as the boats entered the freezing cold of the Southern Ocean, he had sent a fax to Gordon Maguire, his watch leader four years ago on *Rothmans*. It read, 'We have just cranked up the heater,' knowing full well that Maguire did not have one on *Winston*. He kept up the pressure, sending him another a few days before the finish as *Intrum Justitia* headed north, which read, 'Just turned the heater off.'

Intrum Justitia was the first of six boats to finish within eight and a quarter hours. *Yamaha* made it 1-2-3 for the smaller Whitbread 60s before Pierre Fehlmann, competing in his fifth Whitbread, brought the first of the Maxis, *Merit Cup*, home almost seven hours behind in fourth place, an hour ahead of Javier de la Gandara's *Galicia '93 Pescanova*.

The second of the Maxis, Grant Dalton's *New Zealand Endeavour*, winner of the first leg, was sixth, three quarters of an hour behind the Spanish boat. But *New Zealand Endeavour* had had her wings clipped halfway through the leg, when the top eight metres of her mizzen mast snapped off. It happened as the crew were taking down a mizzen spinnaker – the sail went in the water and the halyard wrapped around the mast. The load came on the halyard and the inevitable damage occurred. Yet it was only two days from the finish that *Merit Cup* overtook *New Zealand Endeavour*, when the wind was moderate and the Swiss boat was able to set full sized staysails and spinnakers from her mizzen whereas the Kiwis were only able to use smaller sails.

Winston was next to cross the line early the following morning and claimed a time allowance for going to the aid of *Brooksfield*.

Eugene Platon's *Hetman Sahaidachny* crossed the line almost exactly 14 hours behind *La Poste*, with Platon declaring that they were improving all the time and that they missed out on pre-race practice because the boat had not been finished in time. She did, however, beat the *Women's Challenge*, a boat once again plagued by sail problems.

Dawn Riley said that the crew had 'gelled as the leg went on.' After a time, they stopped asking one another, 'What's your last name and what do you do in real life?' Damaged sails slowed them and when they had to take the mainsail down to repair it, they slipped back into another weather pattern with no chance of clawing back the deficit.

Brooksfield finally made it into Fremantle nine hours after the *Women's Challenge*, the first boat to have to beat her way up the harbour. She had a reefed main and a number four jib set although there was no more than ten knots of breeze. As soon as she was docked, it was easy to see the repairs which had been made – the jockey pole stuck out of the aft deck, where the top rudder bearing used to be. Down below a spaghetti junction of ropes kept the lower end of the jockey pole on top of the floor board that was on top of the bucket and bunk mattress which covered the hole in the hull.

The crew were emotionally charged – there were tears welling in the eyes of watch leader, Andrea Proto, when he said, 'Our main concern was to let the rest of the world know we were all right.' That had been impossible because the navigation station of *Brooksfield* is behind the watertight aft bulkhead and all the communications equipment and electronics were flooded. The only communication means was a hand-held VHF and their EPIRBs.

Fitting the temporary patching over the hole had to be achieved working up to their shoulders in water, and that at a temperature of two degrees Celcius. It was an effort to be applauded and their self-help drew much admiration.

Rescue over . . . and the arguments begin

Escorted by two American Navy ships, *Brooksfield*'s homecoming was dramatic stuff, but the tales of heroism were soured by what others maintained was an exaggerated claim for time redress from *Winston* and allegations from Grant Dalton, whose yacht was on radio duty during the emergency, that he had overheard one skipper pronounce over the radio: 'We are not f****** turning back.' At a heated meeting between skippers and the race organisers called to investigate the matter, Dalton called on the Royal Naval Sailing Association to name names in its report.

The final document fell short of that, but Admiral Sir Jeremy Black, the Race Chairman stated that the broad facts, as reported, were not in dispute, but that the fundamental rule requiring a yacht to render assistance when in a position to do so, had not been broken. 'The yachts that were called on to turn back, did so immediately.' he stated, but the race organisers did win assurances from each skipper that had it been necessary, each would have joined the search.

After reaching Fremantle in fifth place within the 60 ft class, Butterworth claimed that his crew had lost 26 hours in turning back and returning to their original longitude - an allowance, if granted that would have leap-frogged *Winston* two hours ahead of *Intrum Justitia* and lifted her to second place overall.

'That does not reflect reality,' complained Smith. '*Winston* was 250 miles behind us at the time of the emergency and in a very bad tactical position well to the north of the fleet. There is no way they could have caught us up.' Ross Field, skipper of the third placed New Zealand entry *Yamaha* was even more forthright. '*Winston* was 104 miles behind us when she turned back and in a bad situation tactically. We only pulled back 50 miles on Smith so I don't believe they could have overtaken us and am certain they would not have overtaken *Intrum Justitia*. According to my estimates, they should get no more than six hours.'

Dalton, skipper of *New Zealand Endeavour*, which enjoyed a comfortable lead over rivals in the Maxi class despite losing the top section of her mizzen mast during the second leg, had a counter argument. 'I believe that in *Winston* and *La Poste*'s case, they should receive the same elapsed time as the class leaders. Neither skipper balked at returning to help and should be generously rewarded for what they did. Ultimately, the only people who could have rescued *Brooksfield* were other competitors. If it were me out there sinking, I would like to think that someone would come to find me.'

Butterworth said that the time spent beating back against the might of the Southern Ocean was the worst night of his life. 'We had three reefs in the main and a storm jib up. The boat was falling off huge waves and things got a bit scary. Luckily *La Poste* found them. *Brooksfield* was potentially in a lot of trouble. The rudder post had broken inside the boat and was working like a lever on the back of the boat. It would be like someone taking a crowbar to the car's windscreen.'

Of his claim for redress, the *Winston* skipper admitted' 'It will be a controversial decision, but you can't muck about with people's lives. We paid a price and now we just want a fair decision.'

Gordon Maguire, one of *Winston*'s watch leaders, was equally adamant. 'All we want is the time that it took us to go back to *Brooksfield* and return to our position. No more and no less.'

The jury, again headed by Marcel Leeman, took that view, raising the American entry from fifth to second both for the leg and overall by awarding her 21 hours, 28 minutes of redress. It put Butterworth's crew just one minute behind *Intrum Justitia*'s winning time for Leg Two and placed them three hours ahead of Smith's yacht in the overall standings.

Field, was indignant that his yacht *Yamaha* should now be relegated to fourth place overall. 'It's ridiculous,' he stormed. 'I can't see how the jury worked it out. They did not ask for submissions from any of the other skippers, yet we are all involved. It would have been fair if *Winston* had been put just behind *Galicia'93 Pescanova* because that is where she was placed on the race course. Good on Brad for making the claim, but he was in the out-field anyway, well north and in a very, very bad position.'

Smith called the decision 'A farce. Crews should be encouraged to help people in distress, but from the Kerguelen Islands onwards, there was no place changing. Yet the jury thinks *Winston* would have overtaken almost everyone. What has been given to them is almost embarrassing.'

Lodging his own request for redress, Javier de la Gandara, skipper of *Galicia '93 Pescanova* , called the decision, 'Pure theatre. Normally they would have been given 12-15 hours; no more,' he said emphatically.

Ironically, the French crew of *La Poste* who were the ones to reach *Brooksfield* and stood by her crew for 24 hours until a 70 knot gale had swept by, remained third, the same position they were in when they turned back. The jury awarded them 2 days 23 hours and 30 minutes for the lengthy time they lost, giving her crew no favours at all.

Grant Dalton and Chris Dickson were the only people to speak out in favour of *Winston*'s allowance. Dalton hailed it 'A great decision. If *La Poste* had been given more, you would have heard no grumble from me. It is a milestone decision. In future, boats will never hesitate to turn back, and those in distress can be confident that a boat is definitely coming back for them. Nothing should be put above life.'

Dickson was equal in his praise. 'It was a pretty rugged night and we certainly didn't envy them having to go back upwind in 50 knots. They gave all the assistance they could and we are not going to hold anything against them. Certainly the time allowance was generous because I don't think you were going to see them sail past us. The jury made the fairest decision they can and we don't have any problem with it.'

Understandably, Butterworth, saw little wrong with the decision either. 'I think it is a fair result. We have done the right thing by the race competitors and by the race organisation, and we have not been penalised for it.'

Yamaha and *Intrum Justitia* joined *Galicia*'s skipper in lodging an immediate appeal against *Winston*'s allowance. 'As it stands, it will have an effect on the overall result,' stormed Field. But their overtures were all dismissed.

Marcel Leeman, the jury chairman admitted it had been a hard decision. 'We thought it better to go into every detail and all possible material available.' Fellow jury member Graeme Owens added, 'We were primarily concerned with the time spent searching. It was *Winston*'s good luck that she was in different weather conditions to the leaders.'

Far from calming the situation, Leeman's words had a similar affect to petrol on a fire. Johan Salem, shore manager of *Intrum Justitia*, threatened to withdraw his team from the event, while others further down the fleet spoke darkly of turning back at the sniff of trouble, hoping that they too would be lifted up the standings.

In the end, it was agreed that the issue should be re-examined by the jury in Auckland. All the original jury was asked to join the New Zealand jury, but only one, Australian Richard Scott Murphy was able to attend as the others all had previous commitments.

The start from Fremantle saw the return of *Winston* skipper Dennis Conner for the short leg to New Zealand, but his abrupt departure as soon as the American yacht hit Auckland, did little to help his team's cause. Matters were made worse by the fact that co-skipper Brad Butterworth was recovering in hospital from gall bladder surgery when the case was re-heard.

Conner's presence may well have been influential. Instead, the race jury added four hours to *Winston*'s time after deciding that a significant error had been made in calculating the time allowance awarded to the yacht. In a statement, Stavely Roberts said his jury was satisfied that sufficient consideration had not been given to the weather advantage *Winston* had gained once she resumed racing. The change dropped the crew to third 21 minutes behind Ross Field's *Yamaha* and within 1 1/2 hours of the fourth and fifth placed yachts *Galicia '93 Pescanova* and *Intrum Justitia*.

Butterworth said afterwards, 'we are disappointed that the decision has turned against us. We are going to look at the rules they used to turn it round. We are not going to make it easy for them.'

Smith, who returned to England for medical treatment on a foot injury sustained during the leg, countered, 'The reduction is not as much as we had called for. A fair decision would have been to relegate *Winston* to a position just behind *Galicia*, but at least it tightens up the race positions.'

Field, thought that six hours should have been taken from *Winston*'s time, and Juan Vila, *Galicia*'s navigator agreed, 'If they had not gone to *Brooksfield*'s rescue, they would not have passed us. We still feel prejudiced, but it is better than nothing.'

7

LEG THREE *Fremantle to Auckland*
Spectacular finish for the Kiwis

Fremantle, and a great deal of Perth, was out to see the Whitbread Race leave town. More than 600 spectator boats gathered around the harbour entrance and thousands of people lined the shores, particularly around the Ocean Beach Hotel at Cottesloe. Offshore from one of Perth's most favoured watering spots was the first mark of the course, five miles and almost dead downwind from the start.

The fourteen competing yachts had left their berths early, only Chris Dickson's *Tokio* seemed unwilling to leave. Some were out two hours in advance, but Eugene Platon's *Hetman Sahaidachny* was out 24 hours before the start in an attempt to train new crew members who had joined for the race. The amount of Whitbread experience on board had almost doubled with Dale Tremain, who sailed on *Fazisi* in the last race, and Philippe Schiller from *Merit* in the 1989/90 Whitbread, joining her crew.

There were many changes in the crews, some of fundamental proportions. Murray Ross had been invited by Ross Field to join the crew of *Yamaha*, as tactician, to boost its strength. The move did not find favour with navigator Godfrey Cray, who left citing 'personal reasons.' In addition to Eric Tabarly taking over from Daniel Mallé as skipper of *La Poste* to boost the racing perspective, there were four other changes with Halvard Mabire taking over as navigator from Benoit Caignert. With two days to go to the start, America's Cup skipper Mauro Pelaschier pulled out of the *Brooksfield* crew. It was known that he had clashed with skipper Guido Maisto and the move was made for greater harmony.

There was a 20-25 knot south-westerly sea breeze – the Fremantle Doctor was in – and a great deal of apprehension in the air as the two o'clock start time approached. West Australian Premier, Richard Court, was aboard the missile frigate, *HMAS Darwin*, to fire the starting gun and the Training Ship *Leeuwin* marked the other end of the line. Heineken flags were everywhere.

It was a flag which could have caused a disaster to the starting procedure. When the Race Director called for a 'P' to be hoisted five minutes prior to the start, the Yeoman of Signals aboard the frigate set up the hoist in normal naval practice with the 'P' flag inferior to an Answering Pennant. Imagine what the fleet might have done had they seen that. Happily, the disaster was avoided by a sharp eyed Race Director.

The sun shone and the waves were building in the breeze as two distinct groups attacked the starting line on the gun. A group, which included *Tokio* and *New Zealand Endeavour* were at the weather end of the line, close to the frigate; the other group, which included *Galicia '93 Pescanova* and *Winston*, were at the leeward end. *Brooksfield* was the first to hoist a spinnaker but Lawrie Smith calling the shots and Pierre Mas on the wheel, in clear air near the middle of the line, took *Intrum Justitia* to the front of the fleet.

Without their masthead spinnakers (banned on this leg as well as the next and the last) the Whitbread 60s were definitely handicapped against the Maxis and it was not long before *New Zealand Endeavour* with main and mizzen spinnakers pulling, was at the front of the fleet. Pierre Fehlmann took a while to have *Merit Cup* up to full speed, but then moved into second place. The sheer extra horsepower that the twin masted rig could develop was certain to have its effect on the first five mile leg to the turning mark off Cottesloe Beach. Smith, however, was to predict great things for the W-60s, ' The hope onboard is that we can not only lead the Whitbread 60 class, but beat the Maxis again and rob Grant Dalton's *New Zealand Endeavour* of victory in his home port.'

On Gage Roads, off Fremantle, clear wind was an essential for success as Dennis Conner, back aboard *Winston* for this leg, was to find. While the crowds had hoped for a repeat of one of the battles which Conner and Dickson had engaged on these waters six years earlier in the America's Cup, the two protagonists failed to agree and stayed well apart. *Winston*'s start looked reasonable but *Galicia '93 Pescanova* had a little extra speed out of the line and was soon able to blanket *Winston*.

Conner gybed towards the shore and out of the wind. The effect was to put him almost to the back of the Whitbread 60 class as the others ran away in a fine breeze. The two Maxis were first to the turning mark, *New Zealand Endeavour* leading *Merit Cup* by 30 seconds. Then Smith displayed all his small boat racing skills as he held off *La Poste* and *Yamaha* by gaining the inside berth and, being properly prepared, was able to sail away from them on the close reach to the Fairway buoy (once the America's Cup buoy) before coming hard on the wind to clear Rottnest Island.

La Poste had her new skipper, Eric Tabarly, behind the wheel, and the veteran of four previous Whitbreads looked totally at home with his new charge. With navigator Halvard Mabire at his shoulder, Tabarly had soon found the way to get the best out of *La Poste*, but also discovered that the Whitbread 60s, with their windward water ballast tanks full, are formidable competitors on a close reach, and could not hold with *Intrum Justitia*, losing 45 seconds on the three mile reach.

Tokio and *Brooksfield* were able to pull ahead of *La Poste* and behind her came *Yamaha, Galicia '93 Pescanova, Dolphin & Youth* and *Winston* in close order. The all-women crew in their renamed *Heineken* had a massive spinnaker failure - tearing the sail and wrapping the halyards as they approached the leeward mark. They sailed beyond it, gybed and went for the mark without a headsail. They rounded it behind *Hetman Sahaidachny* and *Uruguay Natural* with *Odessa* a minute behind them.

Heineken began to make up time and distance on the reach, overtaking two boats in the process. They had lost time, not only with their mistake, but also in threading their way through the huge spectator fleet. They were not alone in falling foul of this hazard, *Tokio* did it on one side of the fleet and *Winston* on the other. These problems were soon behind all the boats as they came hard on the wind and tacked on to starboard as soon as they could clear Rottnest Island and head south for Cape Naturaliste, the first point at which it was possible to make a break.

It was expected that they would be there at a crucial time, when the westerly sea breeze gave way to a south-easterly land breeze. Chasing the fickle breezes inshore offered an alternative to staying further off the coast and heading straight for the

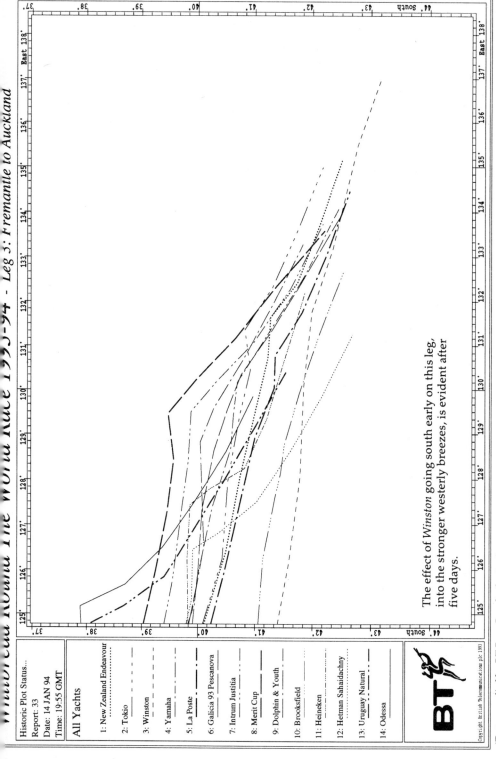

Whitbread Round The World Race 1993-94 - *Leg 3: Fremantle to Auckland*

Historic Plot Status...
Report: 33
Date: 14 JAN 94
Time: 19:55 GMT

All Yachts

1: New Zealand Endeavour
2: Tokio
3: Winston
4: Yamaha
5: La Poste
6: Galicia 93 Pescanova
7: Intrum Justitia
8: Merit Cup
9: Dolphin & Youth
10: Brooksfield
11: Heineken
12: Hetman Sahaidachny
13: Uruguay Natural
14: Odessa

The effect of *Winston* going south early on this leg, into the stronger westerly breezes, is evident after five days.

(Data supplied by BT Race Results System)

stronger breezes well south of Cape Leeuwin. Most opted for the inshore course but *Winston* and, to some extent *Yamaha*, stayed offshore. As they made their way around the south-west corner of Australia, there seemed very little difference in the outcome, but *Winston* was best placed to take advantage of the stronger winds which were expected further south.

The 3,272 mile leg which began in Fremantle was, according to Dickson, 'unbelievably tactical – navigationally tactical – unbelievably so.' 'It was also,' he said, 'a physically and mentally tough race. The first leg was tactically challenging, this one was more so.' The first opportunity for a strategic move was as the fleet approached Cape Naturaliste after a night at sea, hard on the wind in 20-35 knots of wind. 'The wind had been going left, so it favoured the inshore side and we looked good,' admitted Dickson.

At that time, *Tokio* was ten miles to weather and ahead of Ross Field's *Yamaha* which in turn was the same distance away from Dennis Conner's *Winston*. Aboard the red boat, Conner and Butterworth were discussing their strategy, one which they had planned over the previous week with Roger 'Clouds' Badham. The marine meteorologist had spent time analysing the weather pattern off the south-west corner of Australia and had devised a series of alternate strategies for *Winston*, dependent on the exact conditions the boat should encounter when it approached Cape Leeuwin.

Badham had been insistent that if the pointers were right, it would pay to ignore Cape Leeuwin altogether and head south towards the stronger gradient winds and that is what Conner and Butterworth agreed. For a time, it didn't register as good with the race computer, which calculated the distance to the southern tip of Tasmania, but after a day, it was readily apparent that the strategy was excellent and *Winston* increased her lead at every six hour position report until she was 150 miles ahead one week into the leg.

But in the same way that she had gained; through using different weather conditions to the rest, so it was that she was to lose that lead. Two cold fronts brought up the pursuing pack, enjoying brisk north-westerlies on the back of the fronts, so that they were reaching, while *Winston*, ahead of the fronts was in north-easterlies and hard on the wind. The lead diminished rapidly until it had disappeared altogether.

As they crossed the Tasman, Lawrie Smith once again had the best 24 hour run on the leg. This time it was of 401 miles, a whole knot down on the 425 miles he achieved on the previous leg with *Intrum Justitia* to be the current holder of the Omega Trophy. Smith, however, kept to the south of the pack as they headed for the west coast of New Zealand in order to maintain speed and this proved to be *Intrum Justitia*'s undoing. Smith had led the fleet after his high speed charge but he was to slip back to seventh.

It was remarked that Smith was consistently faster than the opposition in the stronger breezes, as the results would show. 'We're probably prepared to sail at a little different angle,' said Smith at the end of this leg, 'instead of going 20 degrees off course, we are prepared to go 30 degrees off, so we can keep a spinnaker up a bit longer – when you've got it up, it's always hard to take it down – this last time, we put a spinnaker up and kept it there while the other guys had jibs up. I don't know why.'

Tokio and *Winston*, together with *New Zealand Endeavour* held on the north side of the fleet and were rewarded, while *Intrum Justitia* holding on port tack into Ninety Mile Beach, came out less well. Two good shifts put Dickson well clear of *New*

Zealand Endeavour, and he was to refer to those when he finished, saying, with reference to Dalton's tactics, 'If they'd followed us three days ago, they would have been here half a day earlier.'

Dickson and his crew spent three days carefully positioning *Tokio* relative to the other Whitbread 60s. 'Each sked saw us alter our strategy. We knew that we wanted to cover *Yamaha* and *Intrum* to the south of us, but we had to keep our eyes on *Winston* and *Galicia* to the north,' he said, adding, 'It probably shows in our track and had we sailed a straight line we might have been better off, but we couldn't let either group go.'

Positioning around Cape Reinga was all important, with a two knot current against the boats, and Dickson took Tokio around New Zealand's most north-westerly point five miles ahead of the Maxis with *Winston*, *Yamaha* and *Galicia '93 Pescanova* in a tight group 15 miles further back while Eric Tabarly's *La Poste* came up to challenge *Intrum Justitia* and take sixth place as they started to close reach to the North Cape before heading down the east coast to the finish.

The wind swung between north-east and north-west during the last 200 miles and jibs gave way to big drifters and spinnakers. *Tokio*, in those conditions, was able to hold off her bigger rival, but there was a seeming inevitability about *New Zealand Endeavour*'s capability of catching the smaller boat; all it needed was the wind to free enough to allow her to set the extra sail area which gives the ketches a huge speed advantage. Dickson probably said it all, 'We could out-sail them. We could out-match race them. We couldn't out-drag race them.' When push came to shove, the sheer power available to Dalton and his crew proved the telling factor.

Grant Dalton's dream was realised at 0317 local time on a Sunday morning. As he crossed the line at Auckland's Orakei Wharf, he let go the wheel of *New Zealand Endeavour* and punched the air with his fists before turning to his navigator, Mike Quilter and gripping him in a bear hug. It was an emotional occasion, but one of the objectives of Dalton's campaign had been realised, he was first into his home port and for a few precious moments that was all that filled his mind.

It was more important to Dalton than non-Kiwis would understand. The pressure on him to perform on this leg dated back four years to when he was beaten into Auckland by Peter Blake. That rankled, particularly since there was some embarrassment about being caught with the wrong sails set when a squall put paid to *Fisher & Paykel*'s chances; but there was much more than that. He had spent thousands of dollars in research to prove that the Maxi would be faster around the world than a Whitbread 60 and this was the chance to prove it in front of those to whom he believed it mattered most.

Not that it had been easy. Forget the 13 days 8 hours 17 minutes and 15 seconds that the leg from Fremantle had taken, when *New Zealand Endeavour* had not been in the leading position except for a few minutes; forget too the whole day that it had taken to sail from Cape Reinga, at the northern most tip of New Zealand; and forget, for a few moments, that Dalton's boat was bigger and had a vaster sail area than Chris Dickson's Whitbread 60, *Tokio*; forget all those things and focus on the last three hours, when for most of it, Dalton's dream looked likely to become a nightmare.

With 30 miles to go, Mike Quilter checked *Tokio*'s position on the radar, it was the last opportunity he would have as the spectator craft were beginning to fill his screen with pinpricks and there were some that could be easily confused with the 'enemy'. *Tokio* was 2.6 miles ahead. The task looked impossible. They had been at it all day and fortunes had waxed and waned; gains had been made and lost, and somehow the smaller boat had been able to repel all their advances, countering any extra speed of the Maxis with some from their own reserves.

Any skipper will admit that luck sometimes has to play its part and for the 'dream' to be realised, Dalton needed that break that only Lady Luck could deal. She did. The wind backed slightly, enough for Dalton to be able to square off and set the gigantic mizzen gennaker from the aft masthead and the ketch's speed went up. Dickson must have looked over his shoulder and realised that something was up when the radar plots of the two boats began to close.

It was, of course, dark. It had been for almost three hours. It was just after midnight and *New Zealand Endeavour* had just passed the Hen & Chickens; Glen Sowry, the tactician, remembered, 'We were a long time hauling them back, but when it freed so that we could set the mizzen gennaker, we began to haul them in.' With the wind aft of the beam, the ketches were able to set sails forward of the mizzen mast and the mizzen gennaker was the biggest sail on the boat, developing the most horsepower and thus extra speed.

The air on deck was tense; and in the navigation station Quilter watched the radar screen until he could no longer be sure which boat was *Tokio*, but he knew that there was a group around the leader and he could see the gap narrowing. On deck, Dalton, on the wheel, was being given his orders – to steer the boat according to the way it was being trimmed so that the greatest Vmg was appearing on the instruments. The sea ahead became a mass of navigation lights, twinkling as they bobbed around in the confused sea cut up by their own wakes.

Slowly, remorselessly, the bigger boat began to wear down her opponent and for all his match racing experience, there was little that Dickson could do. Not that he gave up trying, but there is very little defence against a boat that is sailing two knots faster. As they approached the Rangitoto Channel there were already more than 250 spectator craft around them and that number was shortly to double once they came closer to the volcanic island that gives the approach to Auckland its name.

With three miles to go to the finish, the two boats were 250 yards apart and the gap was narrowing discernibly. The arc lights for television and the photographers' flashes lit up the sails and there was a spectacle as had never before been witnessed in the history of the Whitbread – two boats aiming for a finish and the issue still very much in doubt.

Dickson, four times the world match racing champion, had a battle on his hands that was rather one-sided. Dalton came at him with the bigger boat and eventually, after Dickson had protected his weather, Dalton's tactical team called their skipper to bear off and head for the line. Dickson said later, 'I thought that I had him covered and was convinced when I saw his spinnaker collapsed, but when I looked further aft, I knew it was all up. There was this huge mizzen gennaker still drawing and when it fell in our wind shadow and collapsed, the other spinnaker was drawing again.'

With just over a mile to go, *New Zealand Endeavour* was through. The crowds in the boats were beginning to cheer. They were pumped up by NZTV, one of *New Zealand Endeavour*'s sponsors, and Peter Montgomery calling the action on their radio channel. For a moment or two, Dickson was the forgotten man - a hero until the bigger boat went past.

The scene was set for the finish. Dalton was drawing away with Orakei Wharf in sight. The gun fired as the ketch crossed the line to an incredible cacophony. Fireworks burst in the sky and there was a tumultuous noise from all the boats and people along the shoreline. Even a Whitbread veteran like Simon Gundry (*Ceram-*

co NZ and *Lion NZ*) admitted as he watched with his sons from North Head, that there had never been anything quite like this. And he was right, very right.

When Dickson's *Tokio* finished 2 minutes and 12 seconds later, the cheers were only slightly less. Two of Auckland's sailors had skippered boats to Heineken Trophy wins in the third leg of the Whitbread Race, and, quite properly, were the overall leaders at the halfway stage with similarly large margins in their respective classes.

The finish easily overshadowed the rest of the leg, not that it had been anything but gripping, but there is something very special about the way Aucklanders have taken the Whitbread Race to their hearts. Once every four years, there is an opportunity for the citizens of this extraordinary place to watch a major sporting occasion on the Waitemata, and they make certain that they draw everything from it.

Horsepower was all for the Maxis, so it evidently was to Tabarly and *La Poste*, who was gaining on the three Whitbread 60s ahead. *Winston* was third to finish, just 10 minutes ahead of Ross Field's *Yamaha*, but 2 hours 40 minutes after *Tokio*. Then came another of those finishes for which this Whitbread is becoming justifiably famous.

La Poste was gaining on *Galicia* and finally overwhelmed the smaller boat just short of the finishing line at Orakei Wharf. The big ketch sailed past to beat the Spanish boat in by just 12 seconds – 7 boats had finished within 3 hours and 20 minutes. An hour and a half elapsed before *Intrum Justitia* finished and another three hours until Pierre Fehlmann brought *Merit Cup* across the line.

There was a great welcome for Matt Humphries with *Dolphin & Youth* who arrived at lunchtime to a totally crowded Viaduct Basin. The crowds hardly diminished all day, as those who had been up all night went home, others filled their places. There was a pause of four hours before Guido Maisto brought *Brooksfield* in and then the special cheers rang out two hours later when Dawn Riley and her all-women crew arrived with *Heineken*.

Dawn said that it had been a fun race this time, far different from the previous one of 1989; mainly because *Heineken* had agreed to sponsor the boat. The sponsorship made a lot of differences. 'We all had new foul weather gear and so we were dry. In the Southern Ocean (Leg 2) I had a drysuit top with the wrist seals ripped off - it was left over from *Maiden* – the whole crew is more comfortable. The boat looks better and we have some new sails and gear.

We are no longer worried about the boat falling apart. On the second leg, every time we put a load on anything, we were standing back just in case.' She concluded, 'Having a sponsor behind you makes the crew believe they are actually in the race, not just a side-show hanging on.'

Matt Humphries said that the lack of experience of the young crew (average age 23) on *Dolphin & Youth* was responsible for the boat not appearing at the front of the fleet. 'The average age on Dickson's boat is 31, and Smith's is 39. Most of the guys on those yachts have either done the America's Cup, the Admiral's Cup or the Whitbread – some have done all three. Barring myself, who did the last Whitbread on an old Maxi, none of the crew have had the opportunity to do such events.' As their performance continuously was improving – they finished just five hours after Lawrie Smith – they believed they could make it into the top five on one of the forthcoming legs.

8

LEG FOUR *Auckland to Punta del Este*
A record-breaking run for *Intrum Justitia*

Through a grey sea, churned white by the wakes of 6,000 spectator craft, the 14 competing yachts made a bizarre start to the fourth leg of the Whitbread Round the World Race, 5,914 miles from Auckland to Punta del Este by way of Cape Horn. No less than eight of the boats were over the line early and only six returned to start correctly. It wasn't quite what Lawrie Smith expected to do, but he was conscious of what had happened to his predecessor in the last race. 'Four years ago, Roger Nilson, the initial skipper of *Intrum Justitia*, lost the mizzen mast off the back of his yacht after hooking up with a spectator boat, and we on *Rothmans* encountered several close shaves with over-eager onlookers. Our first aim on *Intrum* will be to run this unique gauntlet in safety, then put the pedal to the metal and head south for the Roaring Forties and continue a sleigh ride through the Southern Ocean.'

At 1300 local time on 20 February, there was 15-20 knots of north-north-easterly wind and the forecast was that it would back slightly, particularly as the boats began to clear the land. There was rain in the sky and it was to fall – not the most pleasant of days for the spectators, nor for the 175 sailors. The line was set off North Head between *HMNZS Wellington* and *HMNZS Canterbury* in an approximate east-west direction with the fleet heading straight into the Rangitoto Channel. Overhead, the sky was thick with 27 helicopters and 19 fixed wing aeroplanes.

With 30 seconds to go, it was readily apparent that some were going to be too early and it could have been of no surprise that a second gun was fired. Brad Butterworth was the first to spin the steering wheel and *Winston* led the flight of premature starters back to the line. Ross Field in *Yamaha* and Lawrie Smith with *Intrum Justitia* were hard on his stern, while Javier de la Gandara was next with *Galicia '93 Pescanova*. Both Pierre Fehlmann in *Merit Cup* and Matt Humphries with *Dolphin & Youth* had to clear themselves from other boats before returning, while Dawn Riley and *Heineken* and the Italians under Guido Maisto in *Brooksfield*, ignored the recall on VHF. Dawn later asserted that she felt that returning through the spectator fleet would be extremely hazardous and she was prepared to accept a penalty, which she thought would amount to 17 minutes, being added to her elapsed time at the end of the leg.

Meantime, a perfectly judged start by Chris Dickson, about halfway down the line in *Tokio*, saw the overall race leader slip clear of the rest of the fleet. For a while, *Tokio* had clear air and undisturbed water and this enabled the Whitbread 60, with her starboard ballast tanks full, to power away from the rest of the fleet. *Tokio* was almost upright, the angle of heel increasing as the water began to become turbulent with the wakes of the spectator craft. It was a polished performance by the *Tokio* crew which gained them a sizeable advantage as they headed, hard on the wind, towards the Eastern Bays north of Auckland.

The City of Sails' boat crazy population were very guilty of making sailing difficult for the competitors. Their own favourite son, Grant Dalton, suffered badly. First he dropped back into Dickson's dirty air and when he was forced to tack to clear that, he was behind *Heineken* and *La Poste* . Then he found himself in the highly turbulent water kicked up by the phalanx of powercraft heading out of the Rangitoto Channel at 12-15 knots. For once, Aucklanders did themselves, and the competitors, a disservice. It is difficult to imagine how bad things might have been if it had been a more pleasant day.

Even so, there were an estimated 300,000 spectators ashore, lining the coast and headlands to gain a view of the fleet beginning one of the most arduous legs. They watched Dickson at the wheel of *Tokio*, with a slight smile set on his face, draw away from the opposition and hang on as long as he dare on that starboard tack before changing the water ballast and tacking out into a heavy band of spectator craft.

He gained a little more over Dalton, who had also had to take a slight knock on starboard after he tacked back and was forced out again by Eric Tabarly in *La Poste*, enjoying some match racing with his almost sistership ketch, but their speeds were down to 8.2 knots, at least a knot and a half slower than they would have been but for the interference of the spectator boats. They had full mainsails and mizzens and *La Poste* tack changed from her number three genoa to a heavy number one, to match *New Zealand Endeavour*, after half an hour. Yet, still Dickson was drawing away.

As the Maxis seemed engaged in their personal duel, the Whitbread 60s which had returned to start correctly were also gaining on them. *Winston* was ahead of *Yamaha*, in turn ahead of *Intrum Justitia*. *Heineken*, caught up unnecessarily in the Maxi match racing, dropped back and was caught by the pursuing pack before they turned the mark boat, *Spirit of Adventure*.

After 7 1/2 miles in the first hour, Dickson went round first, 3 minutes 51 seconds ahead of *Yamaha*; Ross Field picking his way through the spectators better than the rest. 'We made a good recovery,' said Field, 'and then picked up a favourable windshift. We were very quickly back up with the leaders.' *Yamaha* was 9 seconds ahead of *New Zealand Endeavour* and there was another 57 seconds back to *La Poste*.

Even a 90° course alteration, to avoid one boat, didn't stop the charge of *Intrum Justitia* and she rounded fifth, after *Tokio*, *Yamaha* and the two Maxis, with *Winston* another 15 seconds astern. There was a gap of 45 seconds to *Galicia '93 Pescanova* ahead of *Merit Cup* and *Heineken* and then a further minute before *Brooksfield* rounded.

Just before the Italian boat left the dock, one rather inappropriately named crewman, Fortunato Murato, slipped down the companion ladder and cracked some ribs. He was replaced by Lapo Nustrini, an Italian resident in New Zealand, who had been working on the boat during the stopover, but Maisto's crew had already been weakened when three key crew members announced their intention of leaving soon after the boat had arrived.

Uruguay Natural and *Hetman Sahidachny* headed *Dolphin & Youth* at this stage while Anatoly Verba in *Odessa* lost sight of the mark in the press of spectator craft and rounded a full ten minutes after the thirteenth boat. A lack of electronic

Whitbread Round The World Race 1993-94 - *Leg 4: Auckland to Punta del Este*

Historic Plot Status...
Report: 32
Date: 25 FEB 94
Time: 13:56 GMT

All Yachts

1: New Zealand Endeavour
2: Intrum Justitia
3: Merit Cup
4: Tokio
5: Yamaha
6: Galicia 93 Pescanova
7: La Poste
8: Winston
9: Brooksfield
10: Heineken
11: Dolphin & Youth

Intrum Justitia makes a break further south than the rest. The shorter distance to sail and the stronger winds paid dividends for this strategy.

Copyright: British Telecommunications plc 1993

(*Data supplied by BT Race Results System*)

navgational instruments was proving hard for the Ukranians.

There was some fast-reaching to follow on the course east to the Coromandel Peninsula and the Colville Channel, heading for East Cape prior to bearing off to head south into the Pacific en route for Chatham Islands and the Southern Ocean. With the wind increasing on the first night the pace went up so that at the end of the first 38 hours at sea, the leader's average was 15.2 knots from the start.

It was Smith, with *Intrum Justitia*, who had moved into the lead after a 24 hour run of 410 miles. Immediately the challenge of improving on the 425 mile record was on, and with it the tenure of the Omega Challenge Trophy. It was beginning to manifest itself in the British skipper's attack. After a day, he was 7 miles ahead of *Tokio* and 12 clear of *Galicia '93 Pescanova*. *Yamaha* was another 8 miles behind *Galicia* and *Winston* 14 miles astern of her. The first Maxi, *New Zealand Endeavour*, was already 39 miles behind the leader. *Heineken*, in tenth place, was 80 miles behind *Intrum Justitia*, and three miles ahead of *Dolphin & Youth*. The three 'sweepers' were already more than 60 miles behind the British boat.

Then came the breeze which Smith and navigator Marcel van Triest had been looking for, as they had made a definite heading south. It was from north-north-west at gale force, averaging around 35 knots with bigger gusts. The Whitbread 60s began to fly, four of them clocking more than 400 miles in the 24 hours from 0900 local time on 21 February. *Tokio* did 407.7, *Galicia* 412.8, *Yamaha* 413.8 and *Intrum Justitia* established a new world record for a monohulled yacht of 428.7 miles, an average of 17.86 knots.

Knowledge of a high pressure area ahead (which Peter Blake and Robin Knox-Johnston in *ENZA* on their world record breaking passage for the Jules Verne Trophy skirted by dropping to 62 degrees south), forced the Whitbread fleet to take a different course to that which they had planned earlier. This time, the majority of the fleet, with the notable exceptions of *La Poste* and *Merit Cup*, went to the west of Chatham Islands, whereas in the past they have passed well to the east. Speeds were being maintained five days into the race with the leader averaging 15 knots from the start.

The secret of the fourth leg was one of being in the right place at the right time and of careful study of all meteorological information because, in the words of *Intrum Justitia*'s navigator, Marcel van Triest, 'it was all minefields, booby traps and parking lots out there.' 'That was only the theory,' he added, 'in practice, it was blood, sweat and tears.' Every skipper endorsed van Triest's statement about a leg that was penetratingly wet, continuously cold and frustratingly capricious. Game plans, plotted well before the race began, were ditched and then the abandonment of those plans regretted. It was all too easy to be wrong and dreadfully difficult to string a successful strategy together day after day.

From the start, there was no let up and the strong winds began shortly after. It was on the second day out that *Intrum Justitia* capped her own second leg record by 3.7 miles. It was achieved sailing a true wind angle of 150 degrees and with the ballast tanks filled. This was Smith's recipe for success, but one which has an element of risk. 'If you do a Chinese gybe with full tanks, you are history,' he said, and added that it was probably why some other skippers eschewed the idea.

Smith still considers that 480 miles is possible by a Whitbread 60, if the winds hold. It was during this period that *Tokio* broke her spinnaker booms and because of this could not sail as deep as *Intrum Justitia*, with her asymmetric spinnaker tacked to the bow. Dickson believes that he would have been able to match Smith's performance and that he would have gone on the same southerly route, which was to put *Intrum Justitia* into the lead. Lawrie Smith determinedly went that way and was at one time 200 miles further south than any of the rest of the fleet and while many would agree that it was the right way to go as it means sailing a shorter distance, this strategy does not find favour with everyone. Smith, nevertheless led for most of the way to Cape Horn, only relinquishing the lead when van Triest demanded they head north prior to rounding the grey rocky outcrop at the foot of South America.

On the other hand, Grant Dalton argued for a northerly track on the basis that it had been proved historically correct. He subsequently pointed to Tabarly in *Pen Duick VI* who had murdered the opposition in the second race by taking a more northerly route and of the mistake of approaching Cape Horn from the south, as *Atlantic Privateer* had discovered to her cost eight years earlier when she was forced to beat to the Horn and even approached it on starboard tack. 'We race every leg with a pre-determined game plan,' said Dalton at the end of this leg, 'and our game plan is based on historical information – the routes of other boats.'

Brad Butterworth confirmed that he too had studied the weather before the leg and also taken into consideration the experiences of boats in previous races. 'We spent a full week with our meteorologist,' he said, 'but I looked back at which boats had done well before and considered the way we had gone with *Steinlager 2*.' For Brad this time, things did not go according to the pre-planning. What began as a dream of winning, became 'a nightmare that turned into a tragedy. Nothing we did rewarded us, and it wasn't for want of trying,' said Butterworth, 'it just seemed that we were clobbered whatever we did.' The *Winston* skipper, with a new Southern Ocean growth of beard, added, 'We are not making excuses – the crew sailed their best ever – but fate was more than a touch unkind to us.'

It seemed that it was not simply sufficient to have a game plan and sail as hard as possible, there were quirks in the wind that were not predictable and Lady Luck played her part as well. Boats that were relatively close to each other – no more than 25 miles apart – could be sailing at quite different speeds; wind pressure rather than direction makes for significantly different performances, particularly among the Whitbread 60s.

The Southern Ocean produced none of its fierce promises. The wind was only over 35 knots on the second day out, except for the second half of the fleet as they approached the Horn. Dawn Riley said that they rounded with 55-60 knots. 'It blew the wind gear off the top of the mast,' she commented wryly, 'We saw it up to 54 knots before it went, and it certainly blew harder than that.'

Most of the time, the wind was around 15-20 knots and out of a northerly quadrant. Only 20 percent of the time was spent running, mostly it was close reaching with jib tops or genoas, but at least 20 percent of the leg to Cape Horn was spent on the wind, just cracked off for speed. That made it a particularly wet leg, arduously tiring for everyone and energy sapping because of the cold. There was no snow this time, only rain. 'From the start to Cape Horn, it never seemed to stop raining,' said Chris Dickson, 'sometimes it was just drizzle and at others it poured. We didn't get dry until a day out of Punta.'

With 1,500 miles to go to Cape Horn, there was cause for concern aboard *Dolphin & Youth*. Twelve days after the start, skipper Matt Humphries became aware that there were problems with the keel. Two of the keel bolts were visibly loose and he asked the navigator, Stephen Hayles to investigate. Hayles re-appeared on deck with one of the keel bolts in his hand. Chris Ramsden, the on-board boatbuilder, found that there were three loose bolts out of a total of 22.

Enduring the Southern Ocean

Peter Blake, a veteran of five previous Whitbread races and victor of the last marathon four years ago, captured the scene best in his forward to an earlier book, *Ocean Conquest*, the official history to the Whitbread. He wrote then: 'It's very cold; even down below, the temperature is only just above freezing. Large drops of condensation are running back and forth across the deckhead. Your sleeping bag and pillow are damp and have been for weeks. You are wearing all your clothes in your bunk to try and get some warmth in your body. Your feet are still cold after standing in the slushy snow that has built up in the corners of the cockpit.

The noise of the sea running past the hull is like an express train that never stops. The cook is rattling pans in the galley. Only your Sony Walkman headphones and some loud music have allowed you to catch any sort of sleep at all.

Now breakfast is ready and it is time to go. The floor is covered with soggy sails, so better not stand there. Where are your boots? There have been a number of sail changes. They have been moved so you have to hunt for them. And you need a pee — urgently. But someone else is 'there' with others waiting. You ask for a plastic bag. There is very little privacy in anything you do.

With your wet-weather trousers on (soggy) you make your way to the galley for a bowl of porridge, covered with brown sugar and reconstituted powdered milk. Then maybe a pancake or boiled egg, or even better, last night's freeze-dried leftovers. And of course, the first of the never-ending mugs of sweet tea.

Now it is on with the wet-weather jacket (wet), harness line, neck towel (soggy) balaclava and Musto hat with ear flaps (a must). With thermal mittens on and a pair of full-leather sailing gloves in your pocket, you are ready to go.

You slide back the hatch. It's like entering another world. Huge breaking seas come marching up from behind. It's bitterly cold — around −5°C. The watch on deck look worn out, but with a glint in their eyes that tells you they are pleased it is you and not they that are going to be doing the racing for the next few hours.'

That is life in the raw in the Southern Ocean, one of the most inhospitable parts of the world. A place where feet and fingers are permanently numb; where the smallest area of bare skin is attached by frostbite within minutes. Yet, the excitement of running before the full force of a westerly gale in the 'Roaring Forties' and 'Screaming Sixty' latitudes is what draws veterans like Blake to come back again and again. Thirty-three crews in this latest Whitbread had done the race before, many more than once, yet they still can't get enough of it.

Russell Pickthall, a veteran from Conny van Rietschoten's *Flyer*, winner of the 1981/82 race who signed on for his third circumnavigation aboard Lawrie Smith's ill-fated Spanish Maxi *Fortuna*, said, 'The Southern Ocean provides the most exciting sailing conditions in the world. There is nowhere else that guarantees surfing conditions and 30 knots plus runs down the face of cresting rollers'.

The keel bolting system, which designer Rob Humphreys had devised, includes bringing the fin into a shallow centreboard box arrangement and there are two 50 mm diameter high-tensile transverse bolts which ensure that the whole arrangement is 'bullet proof.' It was, however, sufficiently damaged for Humphries to order the life-rafts to be strapped on deck with the EPIRB in a grab bag ready to go at a second's notice and for the off-watch crew to sleep in the companionway. As they sailed nearer to Cape Horn, the crew were able to relax, knowing they were sailing closer to safe waters, but a round-the-clock watch was kept on the keel bolts all the way to the finish. Sufficient water was oozing into the hull that the pumps were kept going permanently.

Approaching Cape Horn, the leaders became aware of a very complex pattern of low pressure areas. There was not one, but seven depressions and threading a way between them was tricky. It was here that earlier planning proved essential. *Intrum Justitia*, which had led from the early stages and was by far the most southerly of the fleet, sharpened up and reversed her relative position latitudinally. It cost her places in the fleet to *Tokio* and *Yamaha* initially but van Triest had convinced Smith that they must go that way.

Eventually, *Intrum Justitia*'s lead reappeared as she came closer to the Horn, overtaking *Galicia '93 Pescanova*, *Tokio* and *Yamaha* in the process and staying ahead of *New Zealand Endeavour* – Grant Dalton's dictum of 'coming down for the Horn' having been correct. *Intrum Justitia* rounded at 1917 GMT on 6 March, almost two hours ahead of *New Zealand Endeavour* with *Yamaha* and *Tokio* together another two hours astern with *Galicia '93 Pescanova* 30 minutes further back.

Merit Cup was next, Pierre Fehlmann racing round the Horn for the fifth time and she was followed by *La Poste*, with Eric Tabarly also racing round for a fifth time. The two veterans had uneventful passages this time but soon after *Winston* went round in 50 knots with Butterworth believing that there might be a chance of catching those in front. That hope disappeared as the wind went right down to three knots as they approached the Strait de le Maire.

The leg finished in the most glorious manner, with a three-day match race over the 1,365 miles up the Argentine coast from Cape Horn between Grant Dalton's Maxi *New Zealand Endeavour* and Lawrie Smith's *Intrum Justitia*; a match which Dalton was extremely keen to win and Smith dismissed as 'unimportant'. Dalton was all too aware that the public image of the race was one of 'first home is the winner', while Smith viewed the odds of a line honours win as practically impossible, 'We were racing *Tokio*, not *New Zealand Endeavour*,' he declared, 'They (the Kiwi Maxi) were a nuisance.'

The banter was more light hearted than before and derived from the way in which *New Zealand Endeavour* had covered *Intrum Justitia* on the long beat to windward, a duel which displayed the relative windward performances of the Maxi against the Whitbread 60 and even then the two skippers were not agreed about it. 'In fourteen knots, the Maxi is faster,' said Smith, 'in fifteen knots, they are even, but in 16 knots and more, we go away.' Dalton believed the change-over point was 14.5 knots, but added, 'they always outpoint us by about 5°.'

New Zealand Endeavour was first into Punta del Este, beating *Steinlager 2*'s record by more than 42 hours, but only 5 minutes 39 seconds ahead of Lawrie Smith's *Intrum Justitia*. Once again, the race had provided a close finish between a Maxi and a Whitbread 60 at night. For those ashore, the outcome was in doubt until the familiar silhouette of the ketch broke out of the darkness, illuminated by the television lights.

As the 84 foot ketch approached the finishing line off the breakwater, another set of lights provided the first glimpse of *Intrum Justitia*, some six-tenths of a mile astern. The two Heineken Trophy winners slugged it out toe-to-toe all the way to the finish. There had been no let up and the balance swung from one to the other in the varying breeze.

Whether the match race stimulated its protagonists to an earlier finish is anyone's guess, but Smith denied that it had. 'If we had wanted to beat *Endeavour*, as a prime concern,' he said, 'we would have done, but we were racing Dickson not Dalton.' Grant Dalton was not sure either, 'We wanted to be first in and if that meant covering *Intrum*, then that was the way we had to go.'

9

LEG FIVE *Punta del Este to Fort Lauderdale*
From Demolition Derby to Doldrums

A pall of unrest hung over Maldonado Bay at the start of the fifth leg of the Whitbread Round the World Race. Four Frenchmen from *La Poste* had been arrested in an incident involving their treatment of a burglar found in their apartment. They were still in jail on charges that would hardly hold anyone in a Western country. Local feeling was against them, but their fellow crewmen made certain that the Uruguayans knew how they felt. As they left the dock, eight members of the crew lined up on the foredeck with their backs to the crowd; as they spun round each revealed a single letter on their yellow tee-shirts. Together, the letters spelled LIBERTAD, the Spanish word for freedom. Happily, their release was secured shortly before the final prize giving at the Whitbread Brewery in London.

Added to the unrest, there was little wind as the 14 boats made their way to the start, with the gradient north-easter giving way to a southerly sea breeze. The sun shone and the crews were happy to be leaving to start the most tactical of all the legs in the race, having prepared themselves and their boats for a totally different type of sailing than they had for the previous one. No longer would they be perpetually cold and wet ; the discomfort of this leg would be forthcoming in burning sun and capricious winds. The latter came immediately.

Weight, or rather the lack of it, was a concern to all the skippers. Lawrie Smith, for instance, decided to go without two of his crew, Markus Mustelin and Rick Tomlinson, saving not only their weight but also that of their food and equipment, a total of 400 kg. Smith also decided to go without many of the spares that had been carried for the Southern Ocean legs and opted for only one spinnaker boom. His gamble was to make *Intrum Justitia* lighter than *Tokio* in an effort to close the gap of 14 hours 11 minutes and 49 seconds with the race leader in the Whitbread 60 class.

Every other boat had made similar weight savings, most of them reducing the amount of food carried – the calorific intake for this leg was generally seen as being 3,500 per man per day as opposed to 5,000 for Leg Four. Ross Field also gambled on provisioning for a 21 day leg for *Yamaha* and began food rationing only two days out from Punta del Este.

Dolphin & Youth's crew had worked for almost the entire stop-over to repair their keel fastening arrangement. They replaced the four vertical bolts from the top of the keel (of which two broke) with ten and filled the gap between the keel and it's 'box' above the hull line with high density material to prevent any movement. There had been a similar amount of work for *Heineken*'s crew to repair the delamination to the hull. Their rudder, of which the bottom one-third was lost, was repaired by

Dawn Riley and the all-women crew of *Heineken* pose for their new sponsorship publicity pictures at Fremantle.
Mark Pepper/PPL

Eric Tabarly at the wheel of *La Poste* off Fremantle.
Mark Pepper/PPL

Working round the clock on *Tokio's* damaged mast in Santos. *Walter Craveiro/PPL.* INSET The ingenuity of the Italian crew of *Brooksfield* amply demonstrated in this arrangement of tensioning lines to keep the shore in place over the hole in the hull where the rudder had broken loose. *Mark Pepper/PPL*

ABOVE *Intrum Justitia* starting the third leg from Fremantle. *Mark Pepper/PPL.* BELOW A wet ride aboard *Merit Cup*. Not even the spray dodger will keep the crew dry in these Southern Ocean conditions. *R Guerrini/PPL*

ABOVE Bowman Ken Hara prepares to trip away the spinnaker as *Tokio* blasts up The Solent towards the West Bramble buoy at the end of the sixth leg. *Bob Fisher/PPL.* BELOW *Yamaha* crosses the finishing line at Dock End, Southampton, to win the 1993-94 Whitbread Race in the Whitbread 60 class. *Thomas Lindberg/PPL*

the Argentinean yard of Astilleros del Estuario.

With the entire fleet prepared, Pierre Fehlmann was first to leave the seawall berth with *Merit Cup*, followed shortly afterwards by Ross Field with *Yamaha*. The rest trickled out into the Bay with the notable exception of the two Ukrainian boats, *Odessa* and *Hetman Sahaidachny*, both awaiting parts and crew from a flight originating in Miami, which had been cancelled. They both left two hours late.

Not that progress was fast. There was but six knots of seabreeze blowing when the twelve boats approached the line, reaching on port tack towards the Heineken turning mark, three and a half miles away off Punta Ballena. Everything that could float was taken out to watch the start and there were crowds along the beaches and vantage points on this sunny day to see the Whitbread fleet leave.

At the windward end of the line, where the Uruguayan frigate, *Montevideo*, was the committee boat, Ross Field was first to cross as the gun boomed out. But he was immediately overtaken by *Tokio* with Chris Dickson setting a masthead reaching gennaker; the bigger sails being allowed on the Whitbread 60s for this leg. Others preferred fractional sails, mainly drifters, and *Tokio* changed to hers. Brad Butterworth had *Winston* well placed and later peeled to a masthead gennaker, the bright red providing a patch of colour on a relatively lifeless scene. Only Gustavo Vanzini with *Uruguay Natural* hoisted a symmetrical spinnaker and sailed, stately as a galleon and just as slowly, straight for the buoy.

It was inevitable that the extra horsepower of the Maxi ketches would prove the undoing of the 60s. They set four or five sails, double the area of the smaller boats, and reached towards the Heineken buoy, sailing a knot faster, with Grant Dalton's *New Zealand Endeavour* taking the lead, hotly pursued by *Merit Cup*. *New Zealand Endeavour* rounded the buoy first, hardening up and tacking on to starboard for the mark off the point at Punta del Este.

Merit Cup followed her round 50 seconds later with Eric Tabarly in *La Poste*, with his depleted crew, another 20 seconds astern. The Maxis were well on their way before a clutch of 60s, led by *Tokio* approached the buoy. Dickson was four and a half minutes behind Dalton and had a minute and a half in hand over Field, but the next three were close together with *Winston* and *Galicia '93 Pescanova* rounding side by side and Smith bringing *Intrum Justitia* up close to their sterns.

The wind had begun to shift back to the gradient north-easterly and Javier de la Gandara and his Spanish crew made good use of the shifts to go to the front of the Whitbread 60 class. By the mark, the whole fleet had bunched up, but began to spread once more as they moved clear of the headland and out to sea. Only *Brooksfield* decided to hug the coast, until *Hetman Sahaidachny* eventually started and went that way too.

Yamaha spearheaded the fleet from *Tokio*, then came the three Maxis with *Merit Cup* leading and *Intrum Justitia*, gradually beginning to claw her way back from a relatively indifferent start. Matt Humphries' *Dolphin & Youth* took a mid-line, between the main group and Brooksfield, and for a while paid the penalty, but two days into the leg he picked up a decent breeze and rejoined the leaders.

Progress for the first four days was anything but good, leading to some concern by those who had been sparse with their food provisioning of the yachts, that was until they met stronger northerlies, which, with the north-easterly going Brazilian Current, made the seas square edged and the going considerably tougher. The conditions, described by Ross Field as 'very rough...and bloody bouncy,' were to take their toll on the fleet.

Just into the fifth day, Matt Humphries radioed that *Dolphin & Youth* had sustained damage sufficient for him to be heading towards a Brazilian port, then 280 miles away. A crack, 1.7 metres long had developed in the starboard side forward (the boats were all hard on the wind on port tack), but on the inside skin only. Taking such remedial action as they could, the Dolphin crew cut up a foam floorboard and bonded it to the inner skin and shored it to limit the damage. Humphries headed for the Brazilian coast, aiming initially for the port of Itajai, where there is a boatyard and hoisting facilities, but eventually deciding on Rio de Janeiro for other logistical reasons.

Eight hours later, *Tokio*'s mast went over the side and with it all hopes of Chris Dickson and his crew winning the Whitbread 60 class. Roy Dickson, Chris's father, reported from *Tokio*'s base in Auckland, 'We don't know what has caused the breakage. Every item of gear was meticulously checked during the Punta del Este stopover.' At the time, they had been disputing the lead on the fifth leg with *Intrum Justitia* and *Yamaha*, beating to windward in 26 knots of breeze with a full mainsail and number three genoa when, with a sickening crack, the mast snapped at the first spreader and Dickson was faced with making the Brazilian coast under a jury rig. His early progress was dreadfully slow, but that was during the hours of darkness – Dickson planned to make an assessment and decide on a destination at first light on the Thursday morning.

The wind increased and the total of the jury rig was that the storm jib and the trysail were set sideways on the stump. *Tokio* was headed for Santos and began to sail at over five knots in 35 knots of wind. The crew were all harnessed on as the motion was frightful and the starboard side 'fence' was down. Back in Auckland plans were underway to make replacement sections for the mast and to manufacture replacement rigging rods. The workshops of Southern Spars were busy, but they would not complete their work until six days after the spar had broken and it would be another day before the entire package was in Brazil. Then there were the Customs formalities to cope with, but Roy had already alerted the New Zealand consulate and emergency measures were in hand. Even in this worst-case scenario, the logistical support was able to cope.

The fifth leg was expected to be a cakewalk, compared with any of the others, but it proved to be both tantalisingly capricious and brutally destructive, anything but the Caribbean cruise the crews believe they were promised. It was certainly the most varied of all the legs, in terms of weather conditions, but all the competitors admitted that bad weather in the warm is far better than bad weather when it is cold.

It opened with light weather, as the boats began to make their way north up the Brazilian coast and turned into a windward slog in heavy seas with 25-35 knot winds and a weather-going Brazilian Current. The square edged seas and the necessity to keep to the pace of the leader proved devastatingly hard on boats and gear and peaked dramatically when *Dolphin & Youth* and *Tokio* were forced to head for Brazilian ports to effect repairs.

In Rio de Janeiro, Matthew Humphries faced the problems of a long Customs clearance prior to being joined by Giovanni Belgrano from SP Systems and Donald Guiden, a freelance boatbuilder. Repairs were effected and *Dolphin & Youth* rejoined the race, but five days down.

Even worse was happening to Chris Dickson with *Tokio* as it was generally agreed that, barring accidents, *Tokio* would have won the race in the Whitbread 60 class, but, now the race, in competitive terms, was over for Dickson and his crew. Nothing deterred, they salvaged the top section of the rig, sailed to Santos, negotiated the purchase of a piece of mast section to increase the height of their jury rig to eleven metres and set off for Vitoria, 425 miles away. It was in Vitoria that *Tokio* was met by a sparmaker and rigger from New Zealand with a seven and a half metre mid-section and the new mast was constructed on the dockside and set up in the boat with the help of a container crane. Turnaround time was just 41 hours before Dickson was sailing *Tokio* away from the dock and back into the race.

The two boats were damaged within four hours of each other, and at the time, *Tokio* was sharing the lead with *Intrum Justitia*. 'We were relieved to hear about that, but knew how Dicko would feel,' said Smith, who had started the leg in second position overall, 16 hours down on *Tokio*, and aimed to narrow this to around ten hours on the fifth leg. The dismasting put *Intrum Justitia* into a 3 hour 37 minute overall lead in front of *Yamaha*.

The damage toll continued while Guido Maisto in *Brooksfield* pulled off the tactical coup of the leg. He chose to sail well inshore and in four days went from sixth W-60 to be second, one week into the race. Lighter sea conditions were responsible for making *Brooksfield* fast as well as her being freed by the wind. The heavy seas took their toll on Grant Dalton's *New Zealand Endeavour*. As the ketch slogged to windward, a patch of delamination, more than a metre long and half a metre wide was discovered on the starboard side and she lost 12 hours while trying to repair the damage. This was achieved by running the boat downwind to minimise the 'panting' of the hull and shoring the affected area with cut up floorboards braced with the metal pipes from cook Cole Sheehan's and navigator Mike Quilter's bunks.

New Zealand Endeavour was then able to beat at full speed on starboard tack, but Dalton admitted, 'Our reservations are in beating to windward into high winds on a port tack, when the starboard topsides would be underwater.' Fortunately the weather moderated, and from Recife onwards, the majority of the sailing was on port tack and downwind.

La Poste also suffered delamination damage on the starboard side as the Demolition Derby continued. Tabarly's crew also used cut up floorboards to effect a temporary repair and made an extra transverse bulkhead to hold them in place, which they fitted between a longitudinal stringer and a rail reinforcement. They still had to ease back when hard on the wind on port tack.

A day earlier, one of the fuel tanks on *Heineken* had burst, swamping the bilges with diesel oil. It meant that the crew was restricted on the amount of electricity which could be generated and thus the amount of water that could be made. A day after the tank had burst, the boat had been fully dried, but the smell of diesel pervaded the boat and the temperature was high – even the sea was at 27° Celsius. 'We had no showers, no fans and no lights at night,' said skipper, Dawn Riley, adding rather ruefully, 'and we installed the fans especially for this leg.'

Heineken's troubles were not to end there; she later broke the tip off her rudder. It was a failure of the repair that had been made in Montevideo and it needed the skipper to dive over the side to clear away the broken part. From then on, *Heineken* had only two-thirds of the designed rudder blade.

Yamaha was in front and very soon *Intrum Justitia* displaced *Brooksfield* for second place after 1,500 miles had been sailed. There were some signs of the south-east Trades beginning to make themselves felt. Pierre Fehlmann in *Merit Cup* was leading the Maxi class, by 60 miles from *La Poste* and *Dalton* had found himself, unusually, in third place after having to run off to make repairs.

Yamaha was then 120 miles off the coast as she passed Salvador and was reaching towards Cape Branco, 350 miles away, on the northern tip of Brazil. *Intrum Justi-*

tia was 15 miles behind as they averaged 11 knots, tight-reaching in 14-18 knots of breeze. It was a time for Field to reflect on whether or not, *Intrum*, out to the east, was in a better position for whatever weather change was to come. 'The others might get the changing pressure systems before us although right now we are holding our own and things are going very well. The seas are relatively smooth although the breeze is ruffling the water. It is warm – a bit like being in an oven – and we can now get on deck in just a T-shirt. After the pounding we took last week, these are very pleasant sailing conditions and *Yamaha* is revelling in them.'

The tight angle of reaching led to a slight moan from Field on the restrictions imposed on the W-60 class by the race organisers. He wanted to be able to use fractional drifters, but said that they were having to 'put up jib tops and are not allowed to have staysails underneath.' He added, 'That has proved contentious and it has been suggested that some competitors have been doing this.' He may have been more conscious of the problem as a reaching spinnaker had been washed overboard during a bad gust a few days earlier.

As the Trades continued, so too did the advance of the Maxi-ketches and a day later *Merit Cup* had moved up to be just 24 miles behind the leader, in third place on the water. Trade wind sailing in a Whitbread 60 isn't the same as it is on a cruising boat. Marcel van Triest, *Intrum*'s navigator reported, 'It has been jib-top, gennaker, jib-top, gennaker...and still the occasional squall for refreshment.' He then began to predict what might happen in the next few days: 'The High on the South Atlantic is much further east than normal, which means the Doldrums have moved further south. Anything could happen in the next few days...'

He proved very prophetic and the two small low pressure areas just south of the Equator caused a lot of change in the Convergence Zone, particularly in the transition between the Trades and the Doldrums.

Winston, further to the east, began to make gains on the rest. With slightly more wind, she was able to sail that little bit faster and Brad Butterworth had earlier predicted, 'With the weather forecast for light air, the boats behind should catch up on the leaders.' He was concerned about *Galicia '93 Pescanova* a mile astern and to leeward and there were to be other considerations as the fleet sailed into the complex convergence zone conditions.

It is all too easy to be simplistic about what did happen and how the pre-planning had been made, but the upshot of it all was that *Yamaha* only paused once during her traverse of the tricky area, and the rest spent rather more time trying to chase zephyrs. Field said that he had deliberately gone further north than the rest around the north-east corner of Brazil and that it had paid. Smith countered that he hadn't dared to go that way because that was where he had lost 150 miles in the previous race. *Yamaha* went through, gaining every time the position reports were issued and her crew could smile slightly as there were very few passing lanes left on the course. Once she was into the north-east Trades and heading for the next turning mark of Barbuda, there was no holding the Japanese/New Zealand W-60.

The treachery of the Doldrums was felt by the rest. Smith said that he watched the progress of *Yamaha*, on much the same line, until Field was 155 miles ahead. 'We were parked and he was going. Every so often we would start to get up to speed and then the wind would die again.' He had to endure the galling sight of *Galicia* pulling away as well, having declared that he would stay close to the others on this leg so that they would not be able to make a break. Yet that was exactly what they were doing.

Lady Luck held for Field and even though the conditions were to favour the ketches in the lighter winds towards the end of the leg, his delight was all too obvious when *Yamaha* crossed the line, first to finish and a long way clear. It was to be seven and a quarter hours before *Merit Cup* would finish and that margin of victory over the bigger boat was only part of the *Yamaha* crew's delight. Three quarters of an hour after *Merit Cup*, it was the turn of *New Zealand Endeavour* and when the Kiwis in the smaller boat beat the Kiwis in the bigger boat, they have something special to celebrate.

Not only that, *Yamaha* had such a lead over *Intrum Justitia* that the best laid schemes of Lawrie Smith really did 'gang aft a-gley'. Smith had declared that his aim would be to reduce *Tokio*'s lead to about ten hours and then go all out on the attack on the last leg of the race. But his plans did not include being beaten in this leg by *Yamaha* by a little over 14 hours. *Intrum* now trailed *Yamaha* by 10 hours 26 minutes 2 seconds in the overall standings and while Smith may have consoled himself that it is the sort of margin he had planned for *Tokio*, the switch around in fortunes was not part of his master plan.

Field, however, said that he had this leg in mind when finalising the design parameters of *Yamaha* with Bruce Farr. His was the last one out of the Farr computer and the designer said that it ought to be six hours faster around the world than any of the others. His calculations came without the benefit of the weather break which *Yamaha* obtained in the Doldrums.

Smith did stretch away from *Galicia*, beating her home by eight and a half hours, and *Winston* also cut back on her lead. Six hours before these two finished, there was just six miles between them, but the Spanish boat was first into a freshening sea breeze and sped away to be an hour and twenty minutes ahead at the finish. *Brooksfield*, without the benefit of masthead spinnakers (all having perished in the stronger breezes of the Trades), was sluggish in the light winds and finished four hours and twenty minutes later, but still ahead of *La Poste*.

When *Heineken* finished, just 48 hours after *Yamaha*, her younger sister went to escort her home. There is tremendous camaraderie between the *Yamaha* crew and the women who have taken over their original boat. There was more too for Dawn Riley and her crew; a special welcoming message to the United States had been delivered from the White House – Hillary Clinton acknowledged their performance on behalf of herself and the President. 'That wouldn't have happened four years ago,' said Dawn, 'it shows that sailing has made an impact.'

A frank revelation

Hell hath no fury like a woman scorned, and Ross Field received a full measure when he sailed into Fort Lauderdale. The former under-cover policeman barely had time to step ashore before running into a $15 million writ served by Nance Frank claiming cheating, defamation and misappropriation of funds following the repossession of her *US Women's Challenge* entry, chartered from Yamaha's New Zealand based operating company, Ocean Ventures Management Ltd.

After regaining control of their yacht back in Punta del Este, Field's management team called in Dawn Riley, a former watch leader aboard Tracy Edwards successful *Maiden* Whitbread crew from the 1989/90 race, to lead a core group of Frank's original crew, including Field's Australian girl-friend Adrienne Cahalan, the navigator onboard. The yacht was re-named *Heineken* at Fremantle, after the Dutch brewery sponsoring the leg trophy prizes, stepped in with the cash to keep the crew in the race.

In her writs, served on Ocean Venture Management, Yamaha, Heineken and the Whitbread race organisers, Frank cited collusion to force her out of the race. But it was not until a few days later when she produced a series of printouts allegedly from her yacht's communications computer, showing the passing of illegal weather information between Cahalan and Field, that sparks really began to fly around the world.

In one transcript dated 10 October 1993, when the fleet was close to the Doldrums, a message purportedly sent from Field's *Yamaha* to the *US Women's Challenge*, then 170 miles astern but upwind, read 'Adrienne. Would you tell me what breeze you have please – urgent. I owe you another. Ross.'

Thirty hours earlier, *Yamaha* had been challenging Chris Dickson's leading New Zealand yacht *Tokio*, then just 2 miles ahead. Within 12 hours, *Yamaha* had run out of wind and dropped to fourth place, 32 miles behind the leader. By 1415 GMT, an hour before the alleged message was sent, *Yamaha* was drifting along at just 3.1 knots and had dropped 80 miles behind *Tokio*. Within a further 24 hours, Field and his crew had fallen back more than 150 miles on the leaders.

According to the transcripts, Cahalan replied 'Ross, I see you are in trouble down there. Best to give you the big picture . . .' and continued to brief the *Yamaha* skipper of their local weather conditions.

In further messages, Cahalan wrote, 'Don't worry, I erase all this correspondence when I send it and when it comes in,' though a day later she asks Field 'Can you tell me how to wipe the receive log. Ross you'd better tell me how to erase this receive log. Ad'

Frank gave some indication of potential wrongdoing by her *US Women's Challenge* crew to the race organisers in Punta del Este after withdrawing her challenge from the race, but the racing rules do not allow crew to protest their own yacht or for the race organisers to protest on grounds other than gross bad manners or sportsmanship. At that time, Frank could offer only one transcript which merely suggested that other messages might have been passed between the two yachts. Certainly, the one message did not warrant disqualification but Ian Bailey-Willmot, the Race Director, issued an official warning to Ross Field and Adrienne Cahalan about their behaviour. Neither chose to reply.

There was also the question of verification. No one believed at the time that it was possible to prove that Frank's photocopied print-out had not been forged. Much later, the sailing case against the two, hinged on this verification issue. Initially, messages sent over the BT satellite system were believed to have been taped after Sandra Hole, spokesman for BT Business Development Services confirmed, 'All messages are taped and held on file for three months before being wiped, but we also hold back-up tapes. It is possible for us to verify any message, but we can only do so under the instructions of the subscriber.' The subscriber in this case happened to be the Whitbread race organisers who owned all the satellite transmission systems, and everyone sat back to await developments.

They were seven days in coming – an extraordinary delay considering the world-wide media coverage that the allegations had attracted – and had all the outward markings of a whitewash.

First came the announcement from BT that it could not verify individual messages, only the billing information. 'BT does not monitor, record or have any access to the content of the messages,' Edward Scott, head of BT's International Promotional Projects confirmed belatedly. The only match he could provide were the number of bytes or letters in each message.

The message coming shortly after from the International Jury was equally dismissive. It ruled that while.' . . Both *Yamaha* and *US Women's Challenge* may have breached Rule 59 which prohibits the receiving of outside assistance, . . . no evidence was presented which would justify calling a hearing under rule 75.1 (gross infringement of rules or misconduct).

The jury appeared to do little to investigate the matter. Neither Field, Cahalan nor Frank was called to admit or deny the charges, or give any mitigating evidence. Significantly, Field had no opportunity to table his counter-accusation against Frank that the transcript files had been tampered with – a crime just as heinous as the original allegations.

Yet the seriousness of the charges against Field and Cahalan could not have been set out more clearly than in the Race Director's memorandum to Stavely Roberts, the Jury chairman. In it, Ian Bailey-Willmot wrote, 'I have in my possession, six pages of transcripts of what purport to be communication between *Yamaha* and *US Women's Challenge*.

I believe that I can present evidence which authenticates the documents beyond any reasonable doubt. I believe that both *Yamaha* and *US Women's Challenge* have deliberately breached (the rules) . . . I am not however sure that the breach is sufficiently serious to proceed under Rule 75 which appears to be the only avenue open to the Race Committee. The allegations have been widely reported in the press and are sufficiently serious to warrant investigation. I am therefore requesting that the International Jury formally investigate the matter and take whatsoever action it considers appropriate . . . '

The International jury replied to the Race Director's request two days later following its investigation of the facts. From the information supplied, it gave consideration of action under the International Yacht Racing Rules and found that no other yachts had lodged protests and that the 'memorandum is, in essence, merely a conduit of hearsay information from competitors. As this information was submitted by interested parties, it does not therefore qualify under IYRR 70.2d.' IYRR 70.2 specifies circumstances by which it may do so.

The conclusion of the jury was that under the racing rules there were 'no grounds under which the jury may open a protest hearing on this information.'

The jury then deliberated on whether it could take action under IYRR 75; a rule concerning 'Gross Infringement of Rules or Misconduct;' and concluded, '*Yamaha* and *US Women's Challenge* may have infringed IYRR 59 (the rule banning outside assistance) but the evidence available is totally insufficient to justify a hearing...'

While the jury took no action, it drew attention to:

i) The seriousness of making such non-proven allegations

ii) The significance of IYRR Part I Fundamental Rule B'

Fundamental Rule B defines 'Competitors Responsibilities' in which the yacht owner agrees, among other things, 'not to resort to any court or tribunal not provided by the rules.' It was a warning shot fired across the bows of any who thought there was something incorrect with the International Jury's findings.

Dennis Conner, skipper of the American entry *Winston* was outraged by the decision not to deal with the case and, unfairly perhaps, heaped the blame on the race committee. After calling for the resignation of Bailey-Willmot, he said, 'I believe that the committee should do everything in its power to enforce the rules, but it doesn't seem to be doing so.'

Field and Cahalan were equally bitter. Having been labelled cheats and damned for life by the jury's ruling, they were robbed of any right of reply, although they were not punished. All Field could do was to call journalists individually, expressing his bitterness at how the case had been handled. 'I am not a cheat. Adrienne is not a cheat and I am very bitter. The issue has taken my eye off the ball for a week when I should be preparing for the last leg. I am very lucky that I have such a good crew who had to take responsibility off my shoulders'.

After another International Jury had inexplicably allowed a yacht in the 1992/93 British Steel Challenge yacht race to motor more than 3,000 miles across the Southern Ocean without penalty, and another had made a mockery of natural justice in its disparate treatment of two crews who turned back to search for *Brooksfield* in this race, here was a chance for yachting to show that it can keep its house in order without any necessity for the legal action that Frank had embarked on. Not only did this jury fail to do that, but it failed those in the dock miserably, and the sport itself.

Instead, it placed a large question mark over the whole International Jury system and use of amateurs at important events like the Whitbread Race. Many within the sport were left asking whether future juries should be nominated independently from national authorities and race organisers by the International Yacht Racing Union and chosen more for their professional legal abilities.

After all, a commercial long-distance race like the Whitbread places substantial stress on the racing rules and existing jury system drawn up to deal primarily with short races and observed breaches. When complicated problems arise such as appropriate redress for crews who turn back to rescue others, or documentary evidence that surfaces months after it has been written, race organisers and juries are given little room to address them adequately.

10

LEG SIX *Fort Lauderdale to Southampton*

Tokio's sizzling finish

It is a recognised fact that coming out of Fort Lauderdale, the only way to go is to stay in the Gulf Stream current, using the magic walkway, with the lift that it gives of between two and four knots; it is accepted that this route has to be taken no matter what the conditions are elsewhere. Quite obviously, neither Pierre Fehlmann nor Guido Maisto had been told what they had to do. Instead of sticking to the usual custom and heading north, they broke out to the east with *Merit Cup* and *Brooksfield*.

The Fort Lauderdale locals laughed and insisted that in two days they would have been left for dead. But they weren't and instead were 150 miles in the lead after five days, according to the computer at race headquarters, and only Javier de la Gandara with *Galicia '93 Pescanova* had made any move to join them, and he too had dropped the fleet by making a rapid easting. It was only after a week at sea, when all the fleet had exhausted the free ride of the Gulf Stream and begun heading more to the east, (also to avoid the worst of the Newfoundland Banks with their thick fogs and icebergs) that any of them began to make any impression on the leaders. It may be said, in hindsight, that had the three leading boats slipped further north when this began to happen, the results would have been very different.

Lawrie Smith in a do-or-die move went further north than the rest. Navigator Marcel van Triest predicted that they would find stronger winds and in sixth place on the water in the Whitbread 60s, Smith needed that something extra. *Intrum Justitia* was rewarded with the stronger winds for a day, but that was all. Going that way also put the boat at greater risk from ice and Smith acknowledged that they had passed a berg no more than two metres away when they were in fog.

At the end of the first week, *New Zealand Endeavour* had begun to hunt down *Merit Cup* and the gap between them had narrowed to just 80 miles. *Brooksfield*, 40 miles south of Dalton's Maxi, had been overtaken, just, but still had *Galicia* 36 miles astern and *Tokio* more than 50 behind the leading bunch of Whitbread 60s. Just 25 miles separated *Winston* from *Reebok* (the renamed *Dolphin & Youth*) with *Yamaha* in the middle. *Intrum Justitia* was another ten miles astern.

One day later and *New Zealand Endeavour* was leading the fleet by 11 miles. Being 120 miles north of *Merit Cup*, and holding 10° higher in slightly stronger breezes, had given Dalton almost 50 percent more speed than Fehlmann, but behind these two the charge was coming from the Whitbread 60s. *Brooksfield* had been dropped as had *Galicia*, their speeds in no way matched the 14 knots of *Tokio*, *Yamaha*, *Winston* and *Intrum Justitia* and only 12 miles covered the four of them in distance from the finish across a front of 144 miles.

Reebok, sailing under her new colours and improved sponsorship from the sportswear company to whom she was now named, reported a close call with an iceberg while sailing in the thick fog and freezing conditions off the Grand Banks of Newfoundland. Matthew Humphries reported, 'We went into an area teaming with icebergs. We sighted two and saw eight on radar. *Reebok* was doing 14 knots when the edge of a berg the size of a house appeared through the fog and missed the boom by, at the most, two metres.' *Reebok*'s crew headed up hard to avoid any more ice which might have broken off from the edge of the berg.

It was at this time that Pierre Fehlmann admitted that he had lost what could have been his last chance to hold his big lead over Dalton. 'We were trapped two days ago when we began to lose speed while sailing on the same course ahead of the fleet,' he said, 'we did not gybe to position ourselves north of it and this manoeuvre cost us at least 50 miles of our lead. This was quite a mistake.' Fehlmann consoled himself that at the time Meteo France's four day forecast still showed in favour of his southern option. He realised that to go north at this point (*New Zealand Endeavour* was 120 miles further north) *Merit Cup* would have lost about 100 miles and he hoped that the long term forecast would get him out of trouble.

With the passing of another day, *Merit Cup* had dropped out of the running, trailing *New Zealand Endeavour* by 85 miles. She had also been passed by *Tokio, Yamaha* and *Winston* who were maintaining the same distance from Dalton's Maxi. *Reebok,* had fallen 50 miles behind the leading three W-60s but was still 30 miles ahead of *Intrum Justitia* – Smith's foray to the north was proving something of a gamble. At times, *Intrum* was the fastest boat on the course over six hours and at others was the slowest.

As May gave way to June, a developing anti-cyclone to the north of the fleet brought with it strong south-westerly winds. It was what the skippers of the Whitbread 60s had been long desiring. By midday on 1 June, *New Zealand Endeavour*'s lead had been eroded to just two miles. *Yamaha* and *Tokio* were neck-and-neck and *Winston* was 22 miles behind them. They were all doing two to three knots faster than the *Maxi* and had established a lead of 100 miles over *Intrum Justitia*, which by now was ahead of *Merit Cup.* Six hours later *Tokio* and *Yamaha* were past *New Zealand Endeavour* and *Winston* was right on her stern.

It was on 2 June that the breeze really filled in strongly and the Whitbread 60s were able to make better use of it than the ketches. At this time *Tokio* came close to claiming the world 24 hour record for a monohull and the others were doing their best to stay in touch. At 0512 on the day she finished, *Tokio* had 118 miles to run with *Winston* three miles astern and *Yamaha* a further six miles back. Rounding the Lizard, *Winston* had hoisted a spinnaker to replace a jib top. Alexis de Cenival, one of the *Winston* bowman, was washed back along the deck by a wave. He stopped only when he hit the boom vang and was knocked unconscious. The quick thinking of Matthew Mason saved de Cenival from going any further. 'Big Matt' grabbed his fellow crewman and dumped him, somewhat unceremoniously down the hatch where Mark Christensen sewed up the gash on his forehead.

The Frenchman had barely recovered from this incident, but had declared himself fit enough to assist in dropping that spinnaker in favour of the jib top, when he was hit again on the forehead by the spinnaker boom. It meant another job for Christensen. When de Cenival arrived at Southampton, he looked as though he had been through a few rounds with a prize fighter and was dispatched to hospital where his fellow crewman's temporary stitching was replaced.

Ross Field aboard *Yamaha* began to regard the strong winds with some circumspection and decided to sail rather more conservatively and forget the chase for the Heineken Trophy for the leg and concentrate on crossing the finishing line safely. When the main halyard of *Yamaha* broke, Field lost some ground on *Winston*, but by then Butterworth was also taking a less aggressive view.

During the last day the fleet had begun to string out once again with *New Zealand Endeavour* 20 miles behind *Yamaha*. Towards the back of the fleet, with 825 miles to go, there were problems again for the all-women crew in *Heineken* with rudder failure for the third time. There were big seas running and skipper Dawn Riley and her crew did not know the full extent of the damage except that they had no steering at all. For a time they drifted, under bare poles, at two knots towards the southwest tip of Britain. Eugene Platon offered to standby with *Hetman Sahaidachny* but Riley refused his offer. It was only when Gustavo Vanzini headed *Uruguay Natural* towards *Heineken* with a spare rudder that the *Heineken* crew were able to accept any assistance.

Handing over the spare rudder provided its own problems. First, the *Heineken* crew had to prepare a floating line with life-jackets lashed to it at regular intervals so that the crew of *Uruguay Natural* could pick it up, attach one of their own lines to it and then send the spare rudder, packed in floorboards and fenders to the stricken craft. That achieved, *Uruguay Natural* continued in the race to Southampton.

It took considerable skill and ingenuity on the part of the *Heineken* crew to adapt and fit Uruguay Natural's emergency rudder to their boat. It involved drilling for the transom fittings underwater and this was achieved by putting the Makita battery drill into a plastic bag which was further sealed with duct tape. Bolts from the generator were sacrificed to attach the rudder bracket to the transom and this was achieved during a brief break in the windy conditions. Attaching the rudder to the

URUGUAY REPLACES THE PARTS THAT OTHER BOATS CAN'T...

stern bracket was an all-hands operation involving four halyards, six guide lines and two of the crew in the water in dry suits before *Heineken* was once more on her way.

A day later, with 377 miles to go, while *Heineken* was sailing at eight to ten knots, the boat rounded up suddenly. The shaft between the rudder and the tiller had broken. Skipper Riley spent one and a half hours in the water tying lines around the rudder so that steering lines could be attached to the outboard end and *Heineken* was then able to proceed at a reduced speed. Food was running out on board and so too was gas for cooking it, yet Riley could joke, 'The sun has just come out for the first time in a week and we will all be skinny when we eventually get to Southampton.'

By then the majority of the fleet was in. The final hours of the last leg of the Whitbread Round the World Race were among the most exciting of the event. As Chris Dickson's *Tokio* spearheaded a trio of Whitbread 60s into the Western Approaches, up the English Channel and into The Solent, she clocked 427 miles in 24 hours, just 1.1 miles short of *Intrum Justitia*'s world record for a monohull set in the Southern Ocean.

'It was exciting,' said Dickson, 'bumping along the South Coast of England at high speed.' In one six hour period, just before the finish, *Tokio* covered 126 miles, an average of 21 knots – enough to bring a smile to any sailor's face. Dickson said, 'One of the crew, because we had only done 96 miles in the first six hours of our best 24, suggested that we should forget Southampton and go for the Omega Trophy.' He added with a smile, 'He didn't last long!'

The *Tokio* crew turned it on for the few spectators who braved the wild conditions in the Solent. Setting a full-sized fractional gennaker (masthead sails were banned for the W-60s on this leg) and handing the jib-top at the Needles, Tokio sizzled her way to the finish, often exceeding 25 knots; a blurred white hull in broken white water, with only the red flashes on the hull and the bright red foul weather gear providing any colour on an otherwise grey day.

Just before the Calshot Spit light buoy, Ken Hara went to the end of the spinnaker pole to trip the 'chute away, with the number three jib already hoisted and one reef in the main for the final five miles up Southampton Water to the finish. The nylon sail flagged out to leeward and was gathered in by the crew as Dickson brought the wheel up to set *Tokio* on a close reach to the finishing line at Dock End, where the QE2 berthed later in the day.

It was a bittersweet triumph for Dickson, who reflected on what might have been, but for the dismasting on the previous leg. 'It's rough out there and things can break. Grand Prix cars crash and its worse for them,' he said, adding, 'It's nice to have finished on a good note – a win is delightful.' He continued, 'The last few days have reminded us what the Whitbread is all about. We had *Yamaha*, *Winston* and *New Zealand Endeavour* close for three days and last night we didn't know if it would be a red boat (*Winston*), a blue boat (*Yamaha*) or a white boat (*Tokio*) that would be first to finish.'

Tokio had totally demolished *Steinlager 2*'s record time for the 3,818 mile leg knocking 4 days 4 hours and 36 minutes off Blake's leg time. *Tokio* completed the leg in 12 days 19 hours 36 minutes 27 seconds at an average speed of 12.41 knots.

Dickson was full of praise for those in his team who remained on shore and of how much work they had done. 'Its nice to have the back-up which they provide,' he said and then went on to talk about the last few hours of the race. 'We just scraped off the rocks off Start Point with a spinnaker and really didn't know where the other boats were because of bad visibility. We were waiting for the computer positions this morning as we didn't know whether we were ahead or behind.' Then he admitted, 'we are all a little weary, but we are glad we are all in one piece.'

It was then the turn of *Winston*, finishing 51 minutes later. Brad Butterworth looked back on the leg he had just completed. 'We started this leg hoping to prove something and it has been mixed fortune for us. We didn't start that well then we got back into the hunt four or five days after the start and then had a great race with the front bunch of boats. Once back with the leaders, it all changed dramatically, with *Intrum Justitia* getting involved and then dropping back. *Tokio* was always there with *New Zealand Endeavour* and *Yamaha* and when it came down to the last three days, they were probably the most exciting days sailing we have had in the whole race. We had our best six hour run in the last 24 hours of the leg.' He went on to predict, 'One day, a Whitbread 60 is going to do 500 miles in a day. It will be a target very much like 400 for a Maxi, but one which will be achievable given the right conditions.'

By the time *Winston* had cleared Customs and made her way into the Ocean Village Marina, *Yamaha* had finished, just 30 minutes behind. There were the inevitable high fives from the crew as the finishing gun boomed across Southampton Water and the smiles on the faces of the crew were to remain there all day. It was lunchtime, but they would have one or two of the trophy sponsor's product before they tackled food.

'We feel very comfortable about winning,' said Field on *Yamaha* with a huge grin, 'but I am stuffed, the whole crew's stuffed, it has been a hard hard leg. There was always the worry of damage and we buttoned back a little bit.' Then he smiled again, 'we are here – we have won it. He added that they knew that they couldn't afford any damage on this leg and had always kept a wary eye on the position of Lawrie Smith on *Intrum Justitia*, their main rival but felt that the 10 hour 26 minute buffer, which they had at the start of the leg, would be sufficient.

'All the dreams have been realised,' said Field, 'but it has been three years of hard work. We had our doubts at Fremantle, but we got better and better. The crew got stuck into it and we made some changes in personnel and I believe they were the right changes even if the decisions were hard to make.' Field reviewed the race in general, 'all the problems are now behind me. We are here, we have finished, that's what we set out to do. Finishing first, that is the icing on the cake.'

Two hours after *Yamaha* had finished it was the turn of Grant Dalton with *New Zealand Endeavour*. The Maxi was accompanied up Southampton Water by the QE2 but there were none of the luxuries of the liner on the Maxi. Grant Dalton had said that he would be the fastest around the world and, indeed, he was. *New Zealand Endeavour*'s 120 days 5 hours 9 minutes 23 seconds was 8 days 4 hours 31 minutes 7 seconds quicker than *Steinlager 2* and this included going slightly further on the second leg when Prince Edward Islands became a mark of the course. It was also 9 hours 45 minutes 37 seconds better than *Yamaha*'s winning time in the Whitbread 60 Class, but it might have been a close run thing with *Tokio* if she had not lost her mast.

'We have achieved everything that we wanted to,' said Dalton, 'we have set a new record and won three legs.' He may have forgotten that his original aim was to be first into every port, but he did win the Maxi class with ease, being 21 hours 41 minutes 24 seconds ahead of Pierre Fehlmann's *Merit Cup* with *La Poste* almost another three days further back.

Next in was Lawrie Smith, who joined *Intrum Justitia* after the double dismasting on the first leg of his Maxi, *Fortuna*, when the European entry was 16 hours down on the leader of the class. He had been forced to gamble on the final leg and it hadn't worked. He had been insistent that he had wanted a Maxi before the race began and, in fact, might have raised enough in sponsorship for a W-60 of his own. Given a reasonable first leg, Smith might reflect on what might have been, as it was, he made light of his second place. 'Four years ago,' he said, 'we were fourth to finish on *Rothmans*. This time round we were second. If that improvement continues, we should by rights win the race outright next time round.' Later he said, 'After 48 hours ashore, I have no desire to do this race again, but in a week's time, who knows!'

Reebok was the fifth of the Whitbread 60s to finish, Matthew Humphries and his crew performing better on this leg than any before, aided by the confidence of full sponsorship. They finished almost two hours ahead of Javier de la Gandara's *Galicia '93 Pescanova*, but the Spanish boat had done enough to take third place overall in the class.

Brooksfield limped home under trysail, having split her mainsail and shattered her spinnaker boom. 'That was the best week of the race,' said skipper, Guido Maisto, about the first week of this leg, when *Brooksfield* had headed off to the east from Fort Lauderdale and led the class. 'And the last week was the worst,' he added, 'because we ended up so far behind our competitors. We've had a strong low pressure system for the past two days and as a result, a lot of damage.'

The first of the two Ukrainian Whitbread 60s, Eugene Platon's *Hetman Sahaidachny*, was eleventh across the line and Platon, who had been strapped for cash from the start, said, 'I think this is a good result for us. You can't compete with ten percent of the budgets of other boats. They could replace sails while we could only put more stitches in ours.

Platon's countryman, Anatoly Verba, was next with *Odessa*, a boat that changed crew with more frequency than they were able to change sails. 'The crew was a lottery,' said Verba, 'we had 19 crew throughout the race.'

Still out at sea and having further problems with the emergency rudder obtained from *Uruguay Natural*, Dawn Riley and the crew of *Heineken* decided to put into Falmouth to meet up with the shore crew and another spare (this one from *Brooksfield*). In three hours the green and white hulled Whitbread 60 was on her way. *Heineken* crossed the line shortly before midnight on 8 June, five and a half days behind the leader. Dawn Riley said of the last few days, 'It has been extremely frustrating knowing that the rest of the fleet has already finished. All the more so when you can only do a few miles a day. It took us six days to cover 700 miles. There was never a time when I wanted to give up and be towed in. Being towed without a rudder is as difficult as having to steer without one – I'd rather be towed back to America. I think this is the most difficult campaign of my sailing career, but I know that two weeks from now I'll be glad I did it.'

The sixth Whitbread Race was well and truly over. The parties in the regatta village were anything but muted. The competitors were reunited once again with their loved ones (and, for some, their bank managers). Euphoria was heavy in the air; reality would set in, but not for some time. The end of a Whitbread race is a unique mixture of pleasure, relief, disappointment and realisation. Pleasure in having completed a major sporting adventure, relief in having come through unscathed, disappointment for those who haven't done as well as they hoped, and realisation that, for all, the adventure is at an end . . . until next time.

11

Satellite Communications
Transmitting information and photos worldwide

Two and a half decades after the world was left spell-bound watching man's first steps on the moon live on television, another miracle in TV transmission took place. Life in the raw on a Whitbread yacht within the icy wastes of the Southern oceans was broadcast.

The Roaring Forties may be much closer to our living rooms than Neil Armstrong's first giant leap for mankind, but the technology to fire images back to land from a fiercely pitching deck was only made possible thanks to the pioneering work of BT.

The mushroom shaped transmission domes, which once dominated ship profiles, now fit unobtrusively below decks on a racing yacht, and were used for the first time to provide 'live' coverage during the 1993/94 Whitbread Race.

The yachts were out of sight from land – and range of aircraft – for much of the nine month voyage, so followers in previous races had to be content with listening to crackling snatches of radio talk from crews describing exciting roller-coaster rides down towering waves, collisions with whales and running an almost endless gauntlet between fog-shrouded icebergs.

During the last race however, we saw it all 'live' in daily TV news bulletins and half hour weekly reports on the race, broadcast to more than 20 countries, using video footage transmitted directly from the fleet.

The breakthrough in technology stemmed from recent advances made in digital video compression technologies. The data required to produce a recognisable picture was reduced to a manageable number for transmission down a 64 kbit/sec communications link. 'It was not the technology of beaming pictures around the world so much as the very limited pathway of the INMARSAT-A link, together with the minimal power available on a race yacht that restricted us.' Edward Scott from BT explained, when the first successful tests were carried out aboard the former Whitbread yacht *Rothmans* during the 1991 Fastnet Race.

Those problems were overcome in the 1993/94 Whitbread by the compression system fitted aboard the yachts. The onboard BT CODEC continually sampled each frame; sending back, via the INMARSAT-A hi-speed data link only those parts of the picture that had errored, because of the yacht's movement for instance. The received file of data was then converted back into picture form by a second BT CODEC at Reuters in London before being transmitted to TV stations around the world via the BT Telephone Tower.

Using what BT called their store-and-forward coding technique, improvements in the quality of the pictures was achieved by coding them at a higher rate – 768 kbit/sec – rather than the 64 kbit/sec INMARSAT link normally allowed. 'It's rather like an egg timer with sand transferring from top to bottom over an extended period without change of form or volume' Scott explained. 'With our system, the bottle-neck is the 64 kbit/sec INMARSAT-A satellite link. The more signals we can send through, the better the picture. As a result, a two-minute clip edited onboard the yacht takes between 12 and 24 minutes to transmit. These clips could be fed via Reuters to almost any TV news editing suite within an hour of them being shot.'

Television producers like Gary Lovejoy, head of sport at London News & Sport who headed the TV pool of race coverage around the world was elated with the results of the BT system. 'For the first time, we carried 'live' bulletins during each leg instead of relying on library footage for the month these yachts take to get from one port to another. It brought the race alive,' he said.

The system had its limitations. There were times for instance, when the geo-stationary satellites hovering around the Equator were too low on the horizon to be 'seen' easily at latitudes higher than 50 degrees south. At other times, the violent pitching motion, particularly on the smaller 60 footers, when they were beating or fine reaching in heavy conditions, made it impossible to 'lock' the transceiver antennae on to a satellite, but enough footage always got through to make up the TV programmes like Meridian's weekly *Sail the World* show.

Another aspect of this technology, exploited by some crews, was the ability to send colour news pictures over the same onboard satellite links to newspapers and magazines. Pictures from two yachts, *Merit Cup* and *Intrum Justitia* were transmitted back to the Whitbread digital Imagebase at PPL's Photo Library at Littlehampton in Sussex for onward distribution to the world's media. Rick Tomlinson, *Intrum's* onboard cameraman took his pictures on a regular Nikon camera and developed the colour negative film during the voyage. He then scanned the selected shots on a Nikon Coolscan digital scanner, compressed the 4-megabyte files, using Adobe Photoshop software running on an Macintosh 165C Powerbook computer, down to around 260 kilobytes, and transmitted them over the telephone link within the INMARSAT-A system directly to PPL and Allsport. Each transmission, costing £7.00 per minute, took approximately 10-12 minutes to complete.

On *Merit Cup*, the crew dispensed with the need to develop film by using a Kodak/Nikon RS2000 camera. This digital camera is a promising development, though it had its limitations. Its limited angle of view, for instance, which turns a picture taken even on a 35 mm lens into one seemingly taken through a 100 mm telephoto, could not give the wide-angle views needed on a yacht, and the maximum 4-megabyte file sizes limited their use to newspaper quality pictures; magazines require much greater resolution from files as large as 20-25 megabytes. The camera system has great potential however, and by the time the next Whitbread race comes round in 1997, these limitations will undoubtedly have been overcome.

The big advantage of the Kodak camera and others now coming on the market. is the speed with which the pictures can be downloaded into the computer ready for transmission. One merely has to plug the camera lead into the back of the computer and it is ready, thus dispensing with the messy business of developing film and the time it takes to scan a negative.

To prove the quality of digital picture transmission, PPL, the official photo agency to the Whitbread Race, sent one of its photographers to Cape Horn to photograph the leading yachts as they sailed round. It is one of the most remote places in the world only inhabited by three lighthouse keepers and their dogs and 24 hours sailing time away from the nearest civilisation at Puerto Williams.

Stationed on the *Galvarino*, a former North Sea oil-rig supply ship, posted to Cape Horn by the Chilean Navy to guard the Whitbread yachts as they went round, PPL's photographer was equipped with an MTI INMARSAT-A suitcase sized portable transceiver. Pictures of the leading yachts were processed onboard and transmitted back to England within an hour of each yacht rounding, then forwarded within minutes via ISDN and modem telephone links to newspapers and magazines as far afield as New Zealand, Australia, USA and Europe.

The latest INMARSAT-A and B transceivers have a duplex capability to take advantage of the fast-expanding ISDN telephone networks which PPL's Whitbread Photo Image base was set up to exploit. By utilising the 64 kbit/sec channel within the system, PPL proved it was possible to transmit front-cover quality 20 megabyte pictures (compressed to 1.5 meg) within three minutes via ISDN instead of the 30 minutes or more it would have taken to send the same file down a normal telephone line. Since the cost of an ISDN call is the same as a regular phone link per minute, this represents a considerable saving.

Sponsored jointly by Whitbread, SCii, the French computer card manufacturer, 4-Sight software, BT, Nikon and Agfa Gevaert, PPL used the ISDN link within each BT Press Office around the world to transmit the race pictures back to the central Imagebase, from where newspapers and magazines like *Yachting World*, *Yachts & Yachting*, *Seahorse*, *Boat International* and *Boating World* in New Zealand dialled in remotely to preview the latest pictures and download a selection directly into their own desk-top publishing systems. For magazines and newspapers without a computer link, Agfa Gevaert loaned PPL their latest Alto sophisticated digital film recorder which allowed them to reproduce multiple original-quality transparencies from the files transmitted from each port, ready for immediate distribution via post or courier.

'For a fortnightly magazine like *Yachts & Yachting*, SCii's ISDN technology solved all our deadline times,' said editor Frazer Clark. 'Suddenly, we can take in high resolution pictures shot on the far side of the world and even Cape Horn, as late as press day. It made the race, and the magazine far more topical.'

Bob Kirwin, Deputy Picture Editor at *The Times*, who had been involved in early digital transmission trials using similar technology at the 1992 Olympics in Barcelona, was just as ecstatic by the quality. He commented on the race pictures. 'The results are outstanding. The quality of the pictures transmitted to us each day were the same as if we had the originals in our hands.'

Another BT first, was the development of an inexpensive satellite-based system to plot and track the yachts around the world. BT integrated GPS (Global Positioning System) data with an INMARSAT-C transceiver on each yacht to produce automatic updates on each yacht. This was used to provide race organisers with updates on the race every six hours which were then made available, not only to the crews via the same INMARSAT-C system, but to the public at large who could poll the information over a fax machine or download the date into their PCs.

A particularly useful feature of the BT Race Results System was to provide the Whitbread organisers with the facility to interrogate a particular yacht, group, or the entire fleet to check their position, course and speed with pin-point accuracy at any time. Skippers agreed that these regular reports, together with the latest weather information from Meteo France, had a dramatic affect on the race. 'It became a hugely exciting game of chess,' Dickson said at the finish. 'With the reports coming in every six hours, we would only be able to snatch two hours sleep here and there. It was like match racing 24 hours a day.'

Closing on the Western Approaches, Dickson thought his crew on *Tokio* had done enough during the night to maintain their 12 mile lead over the chasing yachts, until the BT report came in showing that *Yamaha* had closed to within half a mile. 'It was dark and blowing 35 knots. We were about to gybe and set the small kite, but knowing they were so close, we put the big one up instead,' recalled Dickson after winning the final leg.

The BT system also allowed us to follow close-fought duels like the *Tokio/New Zealand Endeavour* race into Auckland on an almost minute-to-minute basis on a computer graphics display screen. It also gave race organisers a positive check that yachts actually rounded remote marks of the course such as Prince Edward Island in the Indian Ocean.

For crews however, BT's C-sat system as they have called it not only provided them with a direct text/fax link with sponsors and friends, but also with a panic button to alert the race organisers of their position the moment an emergency arose. And if time allowed before the need to abandon ship, a facility within the software allowed the crew to spell out quickly the nature of their problems by selecting one of a number of likely scenarios on a screen menu such as fire, sinking, dismasting or sickness.

'The BT system has set a standard that other race organisers now have to follow,' said *Yamaha* skipper Ross Field at the finish. 'The regular 6-hourly reports certainly made the racing closer – and more exciting!'

12

The sponsorship factor
Commercial returns

For the start of the first Whitbread Round the World Race, the venue was *HMS Vernon*, the Royal Navy's Torpedo and Anti-Submarine School, which included a tidal dock known as Vernon Creek where the boats were berthed. The establishment was closed for summer leave, which allowed the public to visit to view the yachts, and the whole race was organised by volunteer members of the RNSA.

The only sop to general interest was an information office, manned by volunteer WRNS. And somewhere, in a wooden shed, there was a bar where all the interviews seemed to be carried out. It was homely and distinctly low key, despite an interest stimulated by the national press, which viewed the competitors as idiots from another planet. Men, and a handful of women, the tabloids argued, who set off on a venture as foolish as this were signing their own death warrants.

The change, in twenty years, is definitely dramatic, but the result of careful development of the event from what started as little more than a cruise in company to a full-on grand prix ocean race. With that came the attendant circus and Ocean Village Marina in Southampton fully reflected the change. Almost all the boats bore the titles of their major sponsors and that necessitated a shoreside marquee where the real business could be carried out.

Those, however, were just the start of things. There were the sub-sponsors, to Whitbread, of the event, like BT who ran the information bureau, and the official suppliers, like Rockport, who had an impressive shoe shop on site. Moreover, the increase in the number of clothing companies, there to capitalise on the spectators who came to see the boats and their crews, was staggering. Paul Bertie of Ocean World was alone there four years ago; this time he had plenty of competition, although he did agree that the position of his stall ensured that he had more than his share of the best business.

Then there were the bars and food outlets. Whitbread, who run Pizza Hut and TGI Fridays in Britain, were not slow to realise the value of the opportunity to promote these franchises, and, incidentally, to provide much needed refreshment for those who had little time for lunch. With the added entertainment, which varied from the flying of tamed owls to jazz bands, there was something else, other than the yachts, for all members of the family.

Going back twenty years, a charge of 5p each was made for entry to *HMS Vernon* and that money, together with the profits from the sale of race programmes, produced £1,000 for the King George V Fund for Sailors. One hastens to say that this year the commercial profits would have been considerably more than that and that some of the benefit would have gone directly to the competitors; Rockport, for instance, gave each of the competitors three pairs of shoes and those with accredited passes received a substantial discount at Pizza Hut.

The event has grown and with it has evolved the 'Race Village,' one of those factors which failed to make the grade, and thus the event, at the America's Cup in San Diego. The question which has to be tackled is whether the growth and its associated development are good for the event. The answer is that it has undoubtedly improved the stature of the event and in a day and age of increasing professionalism in all sports, its increased public awareness has to be a major improvement. The Whitbread is now an event of global stature, number two to the America's Cup in public awareness, well ahead of the Olympic Games regatta.

That being the case, the more pizzazz that is generated about it, the better it is for our sport in general. There is no doubt that the British Steel Challenge made people aware that one doesn't have to be anything special to race around the world (only to have enough money to pay for it) and that the sixth Whitbread showed, with the help of onboard television each week, that the racing was non-stop (there were those who asked, in Ocean Village before the start, how they anchored for the night) and hard work for all concerned.

They have been able to share the privations of the crews as near first hand as was possible and although they could not feel what it is like to be wet for days on end, they got the drift as the crews were honest, like Clare Francis was all those years ago when the BBC made a film of the OSTAR. It was her frankness on how she felt that made the programme and the similar attitude by all the crews enhanced the coverage of the Whitbread this time.

Many of the sponsors have gambled on the exposure they received through television and they might well have been disappointed. Those sponsors needed the input of the crews. The on-board stories of the race came back in compressed video form through BT via Inmarsat A. The video signals were then expanded and their resolution was better than most news coverage.

There was greater coverage of the race than there was twenty years ago. In the first race, the competitors were asked to report the yacht's position once a week. Organisers and journalists alike waited for each of these, but they were never delivered at a set time and the organisers tended to hold on to them for 24 hours before releasing them, so that there was no sense of immediacy. But then, there were not the sponsors who needed the information to be disseminated.

Today, as was amply demonstrated by the public attraction to the Race Village at Southampton, there is a demand for information, a fact borne out by the heavy demand for details of how to obtain the BT software on CompuServe's sailing forum – the answers came generally from American sources. The Whitbread is now big time.

With more than 2,500 hours of television coverage spread across 150 countries, the 1993/94 Whitbread touched millions of lives. Add to this, the acreage of newsprint given to the race in Austria, Australia, Belgium, Britain, France, Germany, Holland, Italy, New Zealand, Scandinavia, Spain, Switzerland, South America, and the USA where crews or entries hailed from, and the commercial returns become obvious. Before the race, *Intrum Justitia*, though one of Europe's largest debt collection agencies, was a name largely unknown to the public. Their sponsorship of a pan-European entry carrying the slogan 'Fair Pay Please' was done to address that balance, According to Johan Salem, the yacht's team manager, the campaign achieved that with interest.

With the help of a twice weekly racing column in *The Times* from skipper Lawrie Smith and extensive photographic coverage world-wide from crewman Rick Tomlinson, the name and slogan is now seeded firmly with City institutions and the business world. Indeed, even by Auckland, the half-way stage after the crew had set a record pace across the Southern Ocean, the marketing men within *Intrum Justitia* were counting more than £13 million worth of media exposure – a figure they were confident would double by the time the yacht returned to Southampton. Not a bad return on a £3 million investment!

TV figures alone far surpassed the levels of exposure established during the 1989/90 race and compare favourably with other top ranked sporting events. The Whitbread TV Pool packaged 216 hours of regular programming which was shown on terrestrial TV in 22 countries. On satellite, Eurosport, STAR/Prime and ESPN International between them, delivered their race programming to more than 50 million homes.

Highlights include the success of Gary Jobson's sailing shows on ESPN in the United States which regularly achieved ratings of over 1.5 million viewers – to more than justify their prime-time slot. Within the UK, Meridian TV's weekly *Sail the World* show averaged one million viewers a week which put it at the same level as *Rugby Special* and Nigel Mansell's *IndyCar* series.

And then of course there is New Zealand, a nation that has always thirsted on news from the fleet. TVNZ and Peter Montgomery – the voice of New Zealand – have made an enormous contribution to race coverage over the years, and this time they did it with live broadcasts from the starts and five minute peak-time updates slotted in before the main news each night.

BT's input towards improving the TV coverage during this race was significant. Their technology developed to draw 'live' footage from the yachts via the INMARSAT – A satellite links fitted to most yachts, jerked the race out of the Marconi era into the 21st century. 'Over 250 successful transmissions were made from the boats which fuelled the greatest amount of programmes on any yachting event anywhere in the world,' said Edward Scott, of BT. This, coupled with the 3-D graphics developed by TVNZ and the BT race results system, gave programmers the chance to provide comprehensive coverage on a daily basis for the first time.

Even when yachts finished 'out of the frame' the returns were still considerable for sponsors. *Winston* for instance, which set out from Southampton as one of the pre-race favourites, never really matched up to her billing. But RJ Reynolds overcame any disappointment they may have had on the race course to achieve their goals with the help of a sophisticated and well-organised PR machine. An advertising agency called in to design the colour schemes and branding on boat and clothing, made such a visual impact that the message was carried both on TV and 20 or more magazine front covers.The overall objectives behind this cigarette sponsorship was to reposition the brand, then well known in the US, but not elsewhere in the world, further up-market and give it more excitement. The exposure *Winston* received during the race, helped by Dennis Conner's involvement, not only achieved those aims but helped increase sales outside the US.

Another interesting sponsorship deal were the six names behind Grant Dalton's *New Zealand Endeavour.* Each took an equal share in the cost of the campaign, then used the branding and links with the boat to promote their own products or services.While the New Zealand Apple & Pear Marketing Board used the race to promote fruit sales in the US and Europe, the ANZ Bank used the boat as an instrument to help instigate a change within the bank's own management style of operations and strategy. The bank set out to alter their traditional conservative image and management structure, laying off a large number of staff in the process to form a more progressive, leaner and efficient banking group. As part of this campaign, they formed 14 yacht clubs as social centres of support for the boat and encouraged *Endeavour* crew members and ANZ staff to give talks on team-work and use of cutting-edge technology. It did not take long for the analogies between team building on a hi-tech race-winning yacht and the changes necessary to operate a state-of-the-art banking service, became self evident.

Heineken, the leg trophy sponsor, got much of their payback from branded signage on the TV programmes and at the ports which they painted green with flags and banners. For other sponsors, the returns were more subtle. DHL Worldwide Express, for instance, had a specific role to play in getting the Whitbread message across. In their role as official courier, DHL not only shipped the TV tapes from each port to television stations around the world, but came to the rescue of many crews, shipping rudders, fittings and equipment, often without prior notice, to each port.

'By its nature, the Whitbread race presented the organisers with huge logistic and administrative requirements and was the perfect vehicle to demonstrate DHL's global capabilities,' said Doug West, their PR and sponsorship manager. 'Once you add up the countries that the boats come from, the stopovers and the countries that received regular TV packages, the Whitbread had almost the whole world covered – and everywhere there was a DHL office to meet the race's demand.'

Another sponsor pleased with its return was Omega, the official race timer. The Swiss company threw down the gauntlet at the beginning of the race, offering a magnificent trophy to whichever crew covered the most miles over a 24 hour period. First to claim the 'Yellow Flag' was *Yamaha* clocking up 343.7 miles during a fast run through the Trades on their way from Southampton to Punta del Este. During the second leg, first *Brooksfield* then *Galicia '93 Pescanova* laid brief claim to the award before Lawrie Smith's *Intrum Justitia* smashed the world monohull record with a 425 mile burst. The European entry did it again on the fourth stage with a distance of 428.7 miles – an average of 17.86 knots – which *Tokio* came within 1.1 nautical miles of equalling during the final stormy run back up the English Channel to the finish at Southampton. Each of these achievements made headlines for Omega.

Omega, which also presented a watch to the 'man of the match' after each leg, was well pleased with its return. 'The formal reports are not in yet, but we feel that we got a lot of publicity from the race,' said Patrick Buteux, their sponsorship director. 'Throughout the race I was getting calls from places like Jakarta to tell me they has just seen Omega on the television. I found enormous willingness from the organisation to please sponsors. I cannot think of any event where a question or favour was dealt with as promptly as this one.'

Rockport, the official shoe supplier to the Whitbread, used the race as a test-bench for their products as much as for the publicity they gained from the exposure of having the world's top sailors endorsing their specialist footwear. As a result. The company, which was already the No 1 name in the US in the walking shoe sector, due to its exposure in the Whitbread, expects its turnover from international sales to grow from 15 to 50 percent in the course of the next five years.

13

The future of the Whitbread Race
Plans for 1997

No sooner has one race ended, than plans are being made for the next Whitbread race scheduled for 1997. Even before the finish, two syndicates, one from the US and another hoisting a Welsh flag, had already put their entries down.

Winning this four-yearly ocean grand-prix is one motivation, but for many, the real draw remains the Southern Ocean. 'There is nowhere else in the world where you surf for hour upon hour. The sensation beats sex, says one anonymous veteran, keen not to upset his girl-friend. 'It's like riding an express train down a vertical track. The boat hums; spray climbs to spreader height and everyone on deck is willing her on with hollers and shouts, recalls Conny van Rietschoten whose two Dutch yachts, both named *Flyer*, won the 1977/78 and 1981/82 races adding, 'I'd love to sail one of these new Whitbread 60s down there because they are so much faster and more responsive than the IOR designs I sailed.'

A rationalisation of the yachts and a return to Cape Town (not visited since 1985) are on the cards for the next Whitbread, though the rest of the course is likely to remain similar. 'The final decisions will not be made until the Autumn of 1994, but if the political situation allows, Cape Town is a natural choice for the first port of call,' said Ian Bailey-Willmot, the Race Director. This 'tavern of the seas' situated close to the Cape of Good Hope is the last port of refuge before heading down into the Southern Ocean. It makes a better first port of call than Punta del Este, Uruguay which the fleet has called at twice, before and after rounding Cape Horn during the last two races. It also shortens the second leg by a considerable margin and re-introduces two weeks of beating into the course as the fleet head into the south east Trades, encouraging better all-round designs.

The days of the $6 million Maxis were numbered. By Cape Horn, it was generally accepted even by the Maxi crews, that these monoliths had been outclassed in terms of speed and value by the new breed of Whitbread 60s . Three hours was all that divided *New Zealand Endeavour* from Chris Dickson's leading 60, *Tokio* on the first 6,000 mile leg to Punta del Este, and had this new class not been banned from using their mast-head gennakers in the Southern Ocean, there would have been no doubts about the Maxis being beaten boat-for-boat on the third short leg from Fremantle to Auckland.

In Punta del Este, exactly four years to the day that the first concepts of the Whitbread 60 class were placed before the sponsors, Bailey-Willmot declared that they would be the only boats qualified to enter the next race in 1997. 'A one-class race offers a number of benefits,' admitted Bailey-Willmot. 'It makes it easier for the public to follow who is winning and, because of the very close racing, we can chip four to six weeks off the event, by reducing the time – and cost – of having the yachts tied up at the ports of call.'

The Whitbread 60s were conceived through an initiative taken by the English brewery which has sponsored this race from the outset, to develop cheaper, more exciting and safer boats to those encouraged under the traditional IOR rule. Twenty five of the world's leading designers including Bill Lee, Rob Humphreys and David Pedrick, worked in unison with measurers, construction experts and sailors to shape this new class of level-rating yachts.

'We are very pleased with the way things have turned out,' said Bailey-Willmot. 'The top W-60s are very close in terms of speed and we will not make any changes that outclass the existing fleet.'

Having said that, however, the race director would like to see an increase in the freeboard of new designs. 'The present boats are too wet, and an increase in volume below decks would give them a second lease of life as fast cruising boats,' he asserts.

The present ban on the use of mast-head gennakers in the Southern Ocean – placed on the boats following pressure from the Maxi skippers who did not want to be outclassed – will almost certainly be lifted and some restrictions on sailcloth weights may be reduced if this results in more durable sails.

The ban on carbon construction is likely to remain, despite the fact that many skippers complained this time round that the research that went into building the boats out of regular materials so that they matched the strength of carbon hulls, exceeded the cost of using carbon in the first place. Bailey-Willmot remains unmoved. 'That research is now widely known and there is no need to spend that money again. It is very important that we do protect the existing fleet,' he asserted.

He does however see the need to allow changes to the rigs and underwater appendages of the present boats, especially if Cape Town is named as the first port of call. 'The extra windward work is bound to lead to some change in design emphasis and this is the most cost-effective way to keep existing boats competitive,' he says. There is, however, an alternative for the first leg without demanding the long windward passage from south of the Equator; Tristan da Cuhna could become a mark of the course, left to port, and this would keep the boats the right side of the South Atlantic High, so that they would sail largely down wind.

Bailey-Willmot and the Royal Naval Sailing Association, under whose auspices this race has been run in the past, saw no requirement to replace the Maxis with the proposed Whitbread 80 super-class. 'There is no evidence on the horizon of a mega-rise in the world economy. I don't think skippers or sponsors would thank us for replacing one over-expensive class for another, even if the boats were a lot faster than the existing Maxis.'

So the Whitbread Race, now firmly established as the leading global marathon, is set for an exciting future through to the 21st century, putting sailing firmly on the world map as a leading sport.

APPENDIX 1 *Race Results*

Results Leg 1
Southampton - Punta del Este

Maxis:
1. New Zealand
   Endeavour — 24:07:19:02
2. Merit Cup — 24:15:41:39
3. La Poste — 25:18:03:28
4. Uruguay Natural — 28:04:43:37
   Fortuna — Retired

Whitbread 60s:
1. Tokio — 24:10:28:21
2. Galicia '93 Pescanova — 24:20:30:42
3. Yamaha — 24:21:30:22
4. Winston — 24:23:49:25
5. Intrum Justitia — 25:18:03:28
6. Dolphin & Youth — 26:03:22:02
7. Brooksfield — 26:03:35:09
8. US Women's
   Challenge — 27:19:23:45
9. Hetman Sahaidachny — 28:06:32:57
10. Odessa — 40:22:31:39

Results Leg 2
Punta del Este - Fremantle

Maxis:
1. Merit Cup — 25:21:11:43
2. New Zealand
   Endeavour — 25:22:57:23
3. La Poste — 26:04:56:39*
4. Uruguay Natural — 32:08:25:03

Whitbread 60s:
1. Intrum Justitia — 25:14:39:06
2. Tokio — 25:16:39:36
3. Winston — 25:18:40:13*
4. Yamaha — 25:20:27:51
5. Galicia '93 Pescanova — 25:22:10:19
6. Hetman Sahaidachny — 29:19:29:30
7. Women's Challenge — 30:01:29:42
8. Brooksfield — 30:10:28:50
9. Odessa — 33:01:55:27
10. Dolphin & Youth — 33:19:23:25

Combined Times Legs 1 - 2

Maxis:
1. New Zealand
   Endeavour — 50:06:16:25
2. Merit Cup — 50:12:53:13
3. La Poste — 51:23:00:07
4. Uruguay Natural — 60:13:08:40

Whitbread 60s:
1. Tokio — 50:03:07:57
2. Intrum Justitia — 50:17:19:55
3. Yamaha — 50:17:58:13
4. Winston — 50:18:29:58
5. Galicia '93 Pescanova — 50:18:41:01
6. Brooksfield — 56:14:03:59
7. Women's Challenge — 57:20:53:27
8. Hetman Sahaidachny — 58:02:02:27
9. Dolphin & Youth — 59:22:45:27
10: Odessa — 74:00:27:06

Results Leg 3
Fremantle - Auckland

Maxis:
1. New Zealand
   Endeavour — 13:08:15:45
2. La Poste — 13:11:35:27
3. Merit Cup — 13:16:26:04
4. Uruguay Natural — 16:19:36:53

Whitbread 60s:
1. Tokio — 13:08:17:57
2. Winston — 13:10:57:54
3. Yamaha — 13:11:07:59
4. Galicia '93 Pescanova — 13:11:35:39
5. Intrum Justitia — 13:13:15:02
6. Dolphin & Youth — 13:18:10:55
7. Brooksfield — 13:22:04:57
8. Heineken — 14:00:08:10
9. Hetman Sahaidachny — 15:10:53:10
10. Odessa — 16:21:07:38

Combined Results Legs 1 - 3

Maxis:
1. New Zealand
   Endeavour   63:14:32:10
2. Merit Cup   64:05:19:17
3. La Poste   65:10:35:34
4. Uruguay Natural   77:08:45:33

Whitbread 60s:
1. Tokio   63:11:25:54
2. Yamaha   64:05:06:12
3. Winston   64:05:27:52
4. Galicia '93 Pescanova   64:06:16:40
5. Intrum Justitia   64:06:34:57
6. Brooksfield   70:12:08:56
7. Heineken   71:21:01:37
8. Hetman Sahaidachny   73:12:55:37
9. Dolphin & Youth   73:16:56:22
10. Odessa   90:21:34:44

Combined Times Legs 1 - 4

Maxis:
1. New Zealand
   Endeavour   84:16:58:23
2. Merit Cup   85:12:05:12
3. La Poste   87:00:10:48
4. Uruguay Natural   102:03:27:14

Whitbread 60s:
1. Tokio   84:18:55:00
2. Intrum Justitia   85:09:06:49
3. Yamaha   85:12:43:45
4. Galicia '93 Pescanova   85:16:55:01
5. Winston   86:07:54:16
6. Brooksfield   92:17:56:53
7. Heineken   94:10:53:29
8. Dolphin & Youth   96:10:17:59
9. Hetman Sahaidachny   96:11:17:29
10. Odessa   115:19:11:58

Leg 4 Results
Auckland - Punta del Este

Maxis:
1. New Zealand
   Endeavour   21:02:26:13
2. Merit Cup   21:06:45:55
3. La Poste   21:13:35:14
4. Uruguay Natural   24:18:41:41

Whitbread 60s:
1. Intrum Justitia   21:02:31:52
2. Tokio   21:07:29:06
3. Yamaha   21:07:37:33
4. Galicia '93 Pescanova   21:10:38:21
5. Winston   22:02:26:24
6. Brooksfield   22:05:47:57
7. Heineken   22:13:51:52
8. Dolphin & Youth   22:17:21:37
9. Hetman Sahaidachny   22:22:21:52
10: Odessa   24:21:37:14

Leg 5 Results
Punta del Este - Fort Lauderdale

Maxis:
1. Merit Cup   22:12:30:00
2. New Zealand
   Endeavour   22:13:15:53
3. La Poste   23:16:08:11
4. Uruguay Natural   26:07:22:49

Whitbread 60s:
1. Yamaha   22:05:13:50
2. Intrum Justitia   22:19:16:48
3. Galicia '93 Pescanova   23:03:49:04
4. Winston   23:05:10:53
5. Brooksfield   23:09:31:58
6. Heineken   24:05:23:15
7. Hetman Sahaidachny   24:19:10:36
8. Odessa   26:15:42:31
9. Dolphin & Youth   28:03:10:57
10: Tokio   31:01:48:21

Combined times Legs 1 - 5

Maxis:
1. New Zealand
   Endeavour 107:06:14:16
2. Merit Cup 108:00:35:12
3. La Poste 110:16:18:59
4. Uruguay Natural 128:10:50:03

Whitbread 60s:
1. Yamaha 107:17:57:35
2. Intrum Justitia 108:04:23:37
3. Galicia '93 Pescanova 108:20:44:05
4. Winston 109:13:05:09
5. Tokio 115:20:43:21
6. Brooksfield 116:03:28:51
7. Heineken 118:16:16:44
8. Hetman Sahaidachny 121:06:28:05
9. Dolphin & Youth 124:13:28:56
10: Odessa 142:10:54:29

Leg 6 Results
Fort Lauderdale - Southampton

Maxis:
1. New Zealand
   Endeavour 12:22:55:07
2. Merit Cup 13:02:15:35
3. La Poste 13:06:35:59
4. Uruguay Natural 16:09:27:41

Whitbread 60s:
1. Tokio 12:19:36:27
2. Winston 12:20:27:00
3. Yamaha 12:20:57:25
4. Intrum Justitia 13:01:02:49
5. Reebok 13:07:34:21
6. Galicia '93 Pescanova 13:09:28:18
7. Brooksfield 14:01:00:36
8. Hetman Sahaidachny 14:16:49:47
9. Odessa 15:17:40:11
10. Heineken 20:00:14:07

Overall Results

Maxis:
1. New Zealand
   Endeavour 120:05:09:23
2. Merit Cup 121:02:50:47
3. La Poste 123:22:54:58
4. Uruguay Natural 144:20:17:44

Whitbread 60s:
1. Yamaha 120:14:55:00
2. Intrum Justitia 121:05:26:26
3. Galicia '93 Pescanova 122:06:12:23
4. Winston 122:09:32:09
5. Tokio 128:16:19:48
6. Brooksfield 130:04:29:27
7. Hetman Sahaidachny 135:23:17:52
8. Reebok 137:21:03:17
9. Heineken 138:16:30:51
10. Odessa 158:04:34:40

APPENDIX 2   *The Whitbread crews*

Brooksfield

	LEG 1	2	3	4	5	6
Paolo Bassani				*	*	*
Richard Brisius	*	*	*			
Pietro D'Ali	*	*	*	*		
Franco Cattai					*	
Jean Chevalier				*	*	*
Albino Fravezzi	*	*	*			
Jan Hervé	*	*	*	*	*	*
Guido Maisto	*	*	*	*	*	*
Fortunato Moratto				*		
Lapo Nustrini				*	*	*
Mauro Pelaschier	*	*				
Alastair Pratt					*	*
Andrea Proto	*	*	*			
Luca Repetto	*					
Angelo Romanengo		*	*			
Alberto Rizzi					*	*
Stefano Rizzi	*	*	*		*	*
Pierre Sicouri						*
Stefano Spangaro		*	*			
Peter Tans	*	*	*		*	*

Fortuna

	LEG 1	2	3	4	5	6
Guillermo Altadill	*					
Jason Carrington	*					
Anton Corominas	*					
Richard Deppe	*					
Vincent Geake	*					
Neil Graham	*					
Bill Heffernan	*					
Neal McDonald	*					
Shag Morton	*					
Andrew Nash	*					
Russell Pickthall	*					
Dave Powys	*					
Lawrie Smith	*					
Paul Standbridge	*					
Paul Van Dyke	*					
Stuart Wilson	*					

Dolphin & Youth/Reebok

	1	2	3	4	5	6
Richard Bickford	*	*	*	*	*	*
Simon Cunnington	*	*	*	*	*	*
Brendan Darrar		*		*		
Steven Hayles	*	*	*	*	*	*
Matthew Humphries	*	*	*	*	*	*
Toby Isles	*	*	*	*	*	*
Glen Kessels	*	*	*	*	*	*
Gerard Mitchell	*	*	*	*	*	*
David Munday	*		*	*	*	*
Timothy Powell	*	*	*	*	*	*
Spike Ramsden	*	*	*	*	*	
Colin Richardson	*	*	*	*	*	*
Mark Sheffield	*	*	*	*	*	*
Simon Woods						*

Galicia '93 Pescanova

	1	2	3	4	5	6
Guillermo Altadill		*	*	*	*	
Jamie Arbones	*	*	*	*		*
Roberto Bermudez	*	*	*	*	*	*
Javier De La Gandara	*	*	*	*	*	*
Ignacio Eraso	*	*	*	*	*	*
Francisco Fernandez	*	*	*	*		
Paco Fernandez	*					
Marcos Iglesias						*
Antonio Piris	*	*	*	*	*	*
Santiago Portillo	*	*	*	*	*	*
Carlos Sampedro						*
Jan Santana	*	*		*		
José-Maria Torcida				*	*	*
Victor Unzueta	*	*	*			
Juan Vila	*	*	*	*	*	
Juan Zarauza	*	*	*	*	*	

US Womens Challenge/ Womens Challenge/ Heineken

	LEG 1	2	3	4	5	6
Lisa Beecham	*	*	*			
Gloria Borrego	*	*	*	*	*	*
Adrienne Cahalan	*	*	*	*	*	*
Merritt Carey	*	*	*	*	*	*
Susan Chiu	*					
Marleen Cleyndert			*	*	*	*
Sue Crafer	*	*		*	*	*
Nance Frank	*					
Marie-Claude Kieffer		*	*	*	*	*
Vanessa Linsley	*					
Kaori Matsunaga	*	*	*	*	*	*
Renée Mehl		*	*	*	*	*
Jeni Mundy		*	*	*	*	*
Leah Newbold	*	*	*	*	*	*
Michele Paret	*					
Dawn Riley		*	*	*	*	*
Barbara Span	*					
Mikaela von Koskull	*	*	*	*	*	*

Hetman Sahaidachny

	1	2	3	4	5	6
Duro Bebelic				*	*	*
Oleg Belomylstev					*	
Andreas Bolte					*	
Julian Clegg	*					
Sergei Cherbakov	*	*				
Gregory Dowling						*
Yury Doroshenko	*	*	*			
Romuald Favraud				*	*	
Angus Harlow						*
Richard Hewitt						*
David Hooper				*	*	
Konstantin Gordeiko	*	*				
Ivan Kostyuchenko	*	*	*	*	*	*
Vladimir Kulinichenko		*	*	*	*	*
Sergei Maidan	*	*	*			
Zivko Matutinovic			*	*	*	*
John McMullen			*	*	*	
Vladimir Musatov	*	*	*	*	*	*
Piter Ntzhegorodtcev	*	*				
Eugene Platon	*	*	*	*	*	*
Phillippe Schiller			*			
Yury Semenyuk	*	*	*	*	*	
Slava Sysenko	*	*	*	*	*	*

	LEG 1	2	3	4	5	6
Dale Tremain			*			
Clive Tremain				*		
Yury Tokovoy	*	*				
Robert Young						*

Intrum Justitia

	1	2	3	4	5	6
Marco Constant				*	*	*
Knut Frostad	*	*	*	*	*	*
Bo Hansen	*	*	*	*	*	*
Gunnar Krantz	*	*	*			
Tim Kröger	*	*	*	*	*	*
Pierre Mas	*	*	*	*	*	*
Markus Mustelin	*	*	*			*
Roger Nilson	*					
Magnus Olsson	*	*	*	*	*	*
Lawrie Smith		*	*	*	*	*
Paul Standbridge		*	*	*	*	*
Rick Tomlinson	*	*	*			*
Marcel Van Triest	*	*	*	*	*	*
Dominique Wavre	*	*	*	*	*	*

La Poste

	1	2	3	4	5	6
Luc Bartissol	*	*				
Eric Blouet	*	*	*	*	*	*
Ivan Bunner	*	*	*	*	*	*
Joao Cabeçadas	*	*	*	*	*	*
Benoit Caignaert	*	*				
Jacques Caraes	*	*	*	*	*	*
Manuel Castilla	*	*	*	*	*	*
Dominique Conin	*	*				
Patrick Deloffe	*	*	*	*		
Jacques Delorme			*	*	*	*
Michel Desjoyeaux	*					
Hugues Destremau	*	*				
Sidney Gavignet	*	*	*	*		
Marc Guillemot			*	*		
François Le Castrec	*	*	*	*	*	*
Halvard Mabire			*	*	*	
Daniel Mallé	*	*	*	*	*	*
Eric Pallier	*	*				
Nicolas Raynaud			*	*	*	*
Florent Ruppert	*	*				
Eric Tabarly			*	*	*	*

Merit Cup

	LEG 1	2	3	4	5	6
Maurice Adatto			*			
Nicolas Berthoud	*	*	*	*	*	*
Claudio Casiraghi	*	*	*	*	*	*
Etienne David	*	*	*	*	*	*
Pierre Fehlmann	*	*	*	*	*	*
Giovanni Ferreri	*	*	*	*	*	*
Manuel Fischler						*
Jean-François Guillet	*					
Rodolfo Guerrini	*	*	*	*	*	*
Grégoire Jaquet	*	*	*	*	*	
Jean-Dominiq Lavanchy	*					
André Loepfe	*	*	*	*	*	
Pierre Michetti				*		
Hervé Riboni	*	*	*	*	*	*
Gérald Rogivue	*	*	*	*	*	*
Kwan-Min Roubakine	*	*	*	*	*	*
Kaspar Schadegg	*	*	*	*	*	*
Christian Scherrer	*	*	*	*	*	*
Dieter Stadler					*	
Bertrand Seydoux	*	*	*	*	*	*
Georges Wagner	*	*	*	*	*	

Odessa

	LEG 1	2	3	4	5	6
Oleg Doroshenko	*					
Dolph Du Mont						*
Dean Herbison				*		
Stephen Hickey		*				
Conrad Humphreys		*	*	*	*	*
Gennadiy Korolkov	*					
Vladimir Kulinichenko	*					
Igor Kutorkin	*	*	*	*	*	*
Sergei Lastouetski	*	*	*	*	*	*
Alexey Lavzenov				*	*	*
Corin Mackenzie	*	*	*	*	*	*
Mikhail Mikhailov	*					
Nick Nichols					*	
Richar Ott						*
Vladimir Ovtcharenko		*	*	*	*	*
Sebastian Piesse			*	*	*	*
Tony Pink	*					
Tom Thawley						*
Anatoly Verba	*	*	*	*	*	*
Brian Wallis		*	*	*	*	*

New Zealand Endeavour

	1	2	3	4	5	6
Stu Bannatyne	*	*	*	*	*	*
David Brooke	*	*	*	*	*	*
Sean Clarkson	*	*	*	*	*	*
Grant Dalton	*	*	*	*	*	*
Brad Jackson	*	*	*	*	*	*
Allan Prior	*	*	*	*	*	*
Michael Quilter	*	*	*	*	*	*
Tony Rae	*	*	*	*	*	*
Michael Sanderson	*	*	*	*	*	*
Cole Sheehan	*	*	*	*	*	*
Kevin Shoebridge	*	*	*	*	*	*
Glen Sowry	*	*	*	*	*	*
Craig Watson	*	*	*	*	*	*
Nicholas Willetts	*	*	*	*	*	*

Tokio

	1	2	3	4	5	6
Rodney Ardern	*	*	*	*	*	*
Andrew Cape	*	*	*	*	*	*
Jim Close	*	*	*	*	*	*
Chris Dickson	*	*	*	*	*	*
Joe English	*	*	*			
Ken Hara		*	*	*	*	*
Kelvin Harrap	*	*	*	*	*	*
Peter Heck				*		
Gunnar Krantz					*	*
TA McCann		*	*	*	*	*
Matthew Smith		*	*	*	*	*
Ian Stewart		*	*	*	*	*
Jacques Vincent	*	*	*	*	*	*

Uruguay Natural	LEG 1	2	3	4	5	6
Heber Ansorena	*	*	*	*	*	*
Felipe Gomez	*	*	*	*	*	*
Gaston Jaunsolo	*	*		*	*	*
Jorge Jaunsolo	*	*	*	*	*	*
Bernd Knuppel	*	*				
Gabriel Lopez					*	*
Eduardo Medina	*	*	*	*	*	*
Aldo Oddone				*		
Henry Ogando	*	*	*	*	*	*
Dick Pasker		*		*		
Alvaro Pellistri	*	*	*	*	*	*
Daniel Pellistri	*	*	*	*	*	*
Marcelo Porta	*	*	*	*	*	*
Sebastian Raña	*					
Alvaro Robaina			*	*		
Alejandro Salustio	*	*	*	*	*	
Pablo Silva	*	*	*	*	*	
Rafael Sosa	*	*	*	*	*	
Jose Suarez	*	*				
Martin Suarez			*	*	*	*
Gustavo Vanzini	*	*	*	*	*	

Yamaha	LEG 1	2	3	4	5	6
Joe Allen	*	*	*	*	*	*
Richard Bouzaid	*	*	*	*	*	*
Stephen Cotton	*	*	*	*	*	*
Godfrey Cray	*	*				
Ross Field	*	*	*	*	*	*
Greg Flynn	*	*	*	*	*	*
Mark Hauser	*	*	*	*	*	*
Kazunori Komatsu	*	*	*	*	*	*
Robbie Naismith	*	*	*	*	*	*
Murray Ross			*			
Jeffrey Scott	*	*	*		*	*
Steve Trevurza	*	*	*		*	*
Nik White				*	*	*

Winston	1	2	3	4	5	6
Bouwe Bekking	*	*	*	*	*	*
Bill Biewenga						*
Brad Butterworth	*	*	*	*	*	*
Mark Christensen	*	*	*	*	*	*
Dennis Conner	*		*			
Alexis De Cenival	*	*	*	*	*	*
Godfrey Cray				*	*	*
David Hurley	*	*	*	*	*	*
Gordon Maguire	*	*	*	*	*	*
Matthew Mason	*	*	*	*	*	*
Dean Phipps	*	*	*	*	*	*
Matteo Plazzi	*	*	*	*	*	*
Peter Vitali	*	*	*	*	*	*